BACKSTAGE VANCOUVER

BACKSTAGE
VANCOUVER

BY GREG POTTER AND RED ROBINSON

HARBOUR PUBLISHING

To Frances Potter,
for reasons too myriad to mention

To Carole Robinson,
who was so supportive during this epic journey

To the memory of Glenn Albert Potter

CONTENTS

FOREWORD

It always amazes me when people visit my office in Vancouver, look at the hundreds of photos on the wall and ask me where I met Buddy Holly, or Elvis or Louis Armstrong. When I tell them they all came here to perform, they are surprised. Why? From the beginning, this city has had more than its share of theatres, arenas, nightclubs and concert halls. In the early days, we were on the Pantages and Orpheum theatre circuits, which gave citizens of Vancouver the opportunity to see the finest performers in the world right here at home. Some of the performers even decided to permanently move here, like singer Bill Kenny of the Ink Spots.

For decades, performers from Frankie Laine to the Righteous Brothers, from Mitzi Gaynor to Johnny Rivers worked our nightclubs to prepare for appearances in Las Vegas and Reno. We were fortunate to have tireless impresario Hugh Pickett, who risked his own capital to bring us everyone from the great classical guitarist Andrés Segovia to Arthur Fiedler and the Boston Pops, to Harry Belafonte, to Frank Sinatra. During the nightclub era, we hosted entertainers at the Palomar Supper Club, the Cave Theatre Restaurant and Isy's Supper Club, to name a few.

When the nightclub scene transformed in the late sixties, a myriad of venues hosted the new wave of performers, such as Big Brother and the Holding Company, Jefferson Airplane and the Grateful Dead. We had a reputation as one of the best places to play in the world.

Little Richard, born Richard Wayne Penniman, liked to call himself "the King of Rock and Roll," but another title, "the Quasar of Rock and Roll" is probably more apt. Red Robinson Collection

As some of the significant personalities in Vancouver theatre and broadcasting began passing away, it made me wonder, "Where is all the memorabilia going?" There is no repository in our province for this material. Some of these items, from the sheet music, to recordings, to posters, to photographs, are historical documents. The first record company in BC was Aragon Records, owned by former deejay Al Reusch. Al died recently but, thankfully, his daughter preserved all the master recordings he had stored and his original recording equipment.

Jack Cullen passed away and a group of my colleagues worked to save his collection of audio and photographic materials. The same for deejay Monty McFarlane. Jack and Monty were hugely successful radio personalities for decades; they and their collected works cannot be forgotten. Radio and television stations have been tossing out historical material for as long as I can remember. This is a tragedy.

Throughout the years, I have saved all my interviews and photographs, carefully storing them. I hope you enjoy not only my photos and memories but also the memories of my peers and the terrific work of some of my favourite photographers.

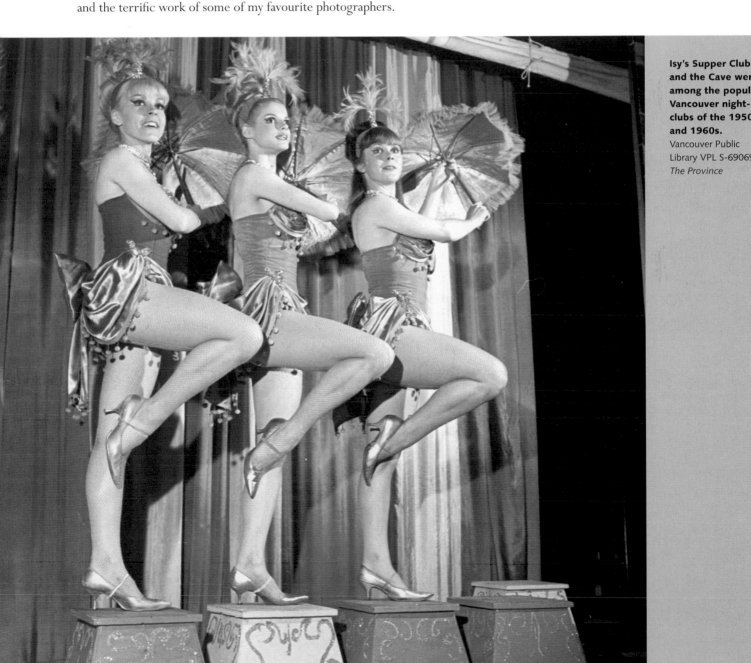

Isy's Supper Club and the Cave were among the popular Vancouver nightclubs of the 1950s and 1960s.
Vancouver Public Library VPL S-69069
The Province

Jefferson Starship, the link between psychedelia and glam rock, featured the vocal duet of Grace Slick and Mickey Thomas at the Queen Elizabeth Theatre in 1983. Dee Lippingwell

Old Blue Eyes made regular stops in Vancouver throughout his long career.
Craig Hodge

Some of us are working on a project to find a permanent home for these valuable items. It is my dream to start a BC Entertainment Museum, whether as a stand-alone institution or part of another museum. Britain, France and the United States preserve their entertainment heritage—why are we so far behind?

It is with these thoughts in mind that Greg Potter and I came up with the concept for this book. It is my belief that, if I can make more people aware of our rich entertainment history, we will collectively take strides toward keeping it.

It is impossible to mention every artist who has graced our stages because the list looks like the phone book. It is also an ongoing story with so much more to come. I know you will be entertained by reading *Backstage Vancouver* because it contains stories of many of the world's most well-known personalities. Enjoy.

—*Red Robinson*

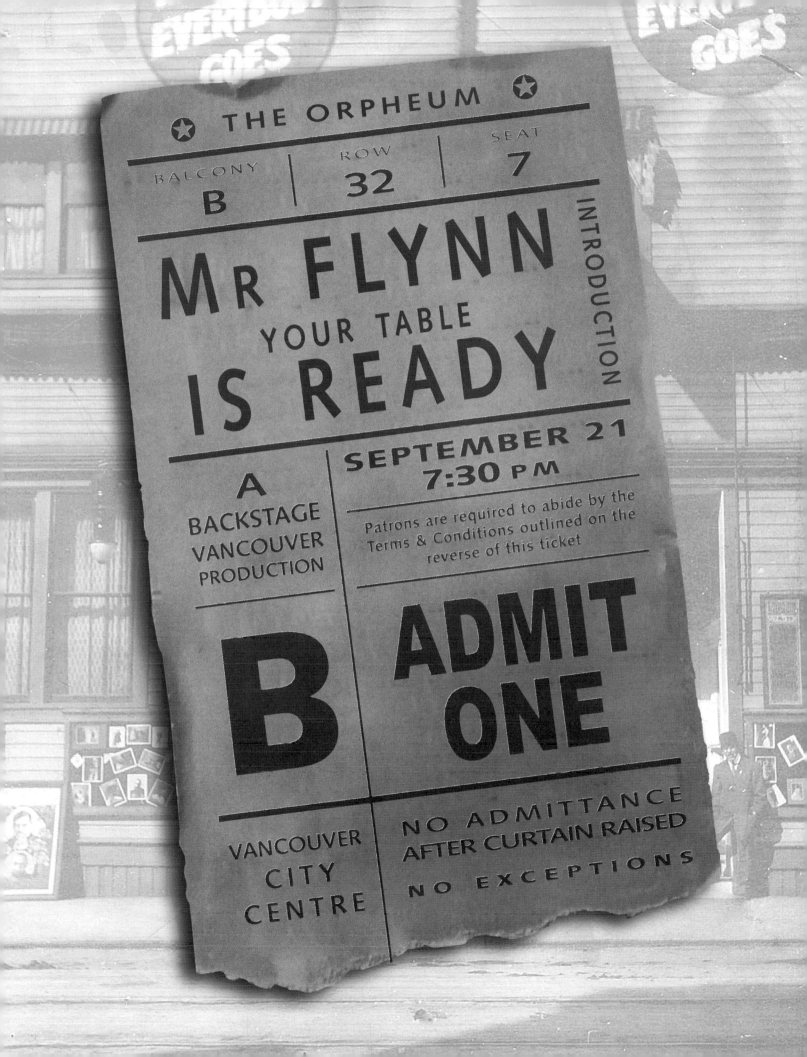

BACKSTAGE VANCOUVER

Elvis Presley's appearance at Vancouver's Empire Stadium on August 31, 1957, was a turning point in the musical history of the city. Red Robinson Collection

Most people are unaware that Boris Karloff worked construction on the Pacific National Exhibition. Or that Coquitlam's Steelhead Lodge, a secluded fishing retreat, was frequented by the likes of Clark Gable and Kim Novak, whose surnames grace street signs in the River Springs neighbourhood to this day. Celebrated French stage-and-screen star Sarah Bernhardt also came for the fishing, while African-American opera singer Marian Anderson fell in love with hockey. Comedians Jack Benny and Dick Martin met their future wives in Vancouver and swashbuckling actor Errol Flynn met his maker. When the latter arrived at the Vancouver City Morgue, through the back door, his body was greeted by a handwritten note on the examination slab that announced, "Mr. Flynn, your table is ready."

City fathers were appalled when Elvis Presley fans tore apart Empire Stadium but Presley manager Colonel Tom Parker was delighted. Bing Crosby lent a hand to opening the Sunset Community Centre because he was "one of the good ones"; jazz master Louis Armstrong was denied rooms at Vancouver's upscale hotels because he was "one of the coloured ones." The Who's Keith Moon managed to get a room, despite his well-known penchant for destroying them, and promptly purchased a pet piranha to keep in the bathtub, entertaining bandmate John Entwistle by trying to "tickle its nose."

Actor David Duchovny considered Vancouver too wet, so he had his TV show, *The X-Files,* moved to Los Angeles. Blind Melon singer Shannon Hoon considered a Vancouver audience too dry, so he urinated on them. Rock band Bon Jovi titled its zillion-selling 1986 album *Slippery When Wet* after seeing the phrase tattooed on the inner thigh of a local stripper. Heavy-metal heads Mötley Crüe, who recorded the multiplatinum *Dr. Feelgood* in Vancouver with local producer Bob Rock, also found inspiration in the city's exotic-dancing establishments—drummer Tommy Lee married a local peeler (yes, prior to Pamela Anderson).

On September 22, 1948, Bing Crosby appeared at the sod turning ceremony of East Vancouver's Sunset Memorial Centre, for which he raised significant funds. Vancouver Public Library VPL S-60081 *The Province*

The *X-Files*, the popular 1990s television show starring David Duchovny (left) and Gillian Anderson, was filmed in Vancouver for five seasons. Wayne Leidenfrost *The Province*

Golfing was one of Vancouver's many attractions for Clark Gable, who was a regular guest at Coquitlam's Steelhead Lodge. City of Vancouver Archives CVA 99-2790

BACKSTAGE VANCOUVER

Playboy playmate Dorothy Stratten was working at a Vancouver Dairy Queen when she was discovered by Paul Snider, her future promoter, husband, and murderer.

Bill Keay *Vancouver Sun*

These are but a few of the off-the-cuff anecdotes vividly recalled (and invariably revised) by Vancouver night owls, celebrity hounds, star gazers, gossip columnists, autograph-seekers and showbiz insiders at the mere drop of a name. Of course, in addition to attracting famous folk over the past century, the city has also provided a springboard to stardom for scores of others, including *The Jack Benny Program*'s Mary Livingstone, *Perry Mason*'s Raymond Burr, *The Munsters*' Yvonne De Carlo, *Star Trek*'s James "Scotty" Doohan, *Quincy*'s Robert Ito, *The Beachcombers*' Bruno Gerussi, *Twin Peaks*' Michael Ontkean, *Beverly Hills 90210*'s Jason Priestley, *Roseanne*'s Sarah Chalke, *Ally McBeal*'s Gil Bellows and *Sex and the City*'s Kim Cattrall; *A Walk in the Sun*'s John Ireland, *Valley of the Dolls*' Barbara Parkins, *Little Big Man*'s Chief Dan George, Cheech and Chong's Tommy Chong, *Back to the Future*'s Michael J. Fox, *Star Wars*' Hayden Christensen, *Saving Private Ryan*'s Barry Pepper and *The Matrix*'s Carrie-Anne Moss; scientist and environmentalist

Impresario Hugh Pickett served as Vancouver's pipeline to the stars while running Famous Artists, Vancouver's premier booking agency, from the 1940s to the mid-1980s. Bill Keay *Vancouver Sun*

BACKSTAGE VANCOUVER

David Suzuki and CNN Gulf War correspondent Peter Kent; rockers Bachman-Turner Overdrive, Loverboy and Nickelback; singers Terry Jacks, Bryan Adams, k.d. lang, Sarah McLachlan, Michael Bublé and Bif Naked; music producers David Foster, Bruce Fairbairn and Bob Rock; and *Playboy* Playmates Dorothy Stratten, Kimberly Conrad and Pamela Anderson.

Legendary Vancouver impresario Hugh Pickett, whose Famous Artists agency was the city's premier talent broker from the 1940s to the mid-1980s, not only booked but also befriended many of the biggest names in 20th-century show business. At 91, he speaks passionately but never patronizingly of the ones whose company he genuinely enjoyed, yet is equally blunt and dismissive when discussing those he couldn't stand (but tolerated all the same). Recalling a coincidental encounter from the mid-1940s, Pickett captures the essence of Vancouver's unique rapport with celebrities, then as now.

"I remember looking in a window at the Hudson's Bay store and there was a good-looking man and a gorgeous woman standing next to me. It was Joan Crawford. I thought to myself, 'What the hell is she doing here?' So, like an idiot, I went up to her and said, 'Oh, Miss Crawford, it's so nice to have you in Vancouver.' Well, she shot back, 'I'm not Miss Crawford!' I said, 'Oh, I'm terribly sorry,' and she said, 'Just a minute,' and looked around to make sure nobody else on the street had heard anything. Then she whispered, 'Yes, I am Joan Crawford but I don't want it to be known.' I said, 'Well, I'm not going to ask you for an autograph; that's not what I'm about. I just wanted to say thanks for all you've done for the industry.' She was terribly nice about it all. She was here for only one day and this was when she was at her peak. But she was on a holiday and didn't want a lot of people around her. And she wanted you to know that. Besides, she shouldn't have been with that guy. We never heard another thing about him."

Vancouver was, and still is, accommodating that way. Stars can walk down the street or wander into shops and restaurants without being overly harassed. Many have second homes here, including Kurt Russell and Goldie Hawn, and some, such as

Newlywed crooner Frankie Laine and wife Nan Grey view Vancouver from Grouse Mountain in 1951. *Vancouver Sun*

Michael Moriarty, have relocated permanently, finding the two-hour air commute to Los Angeles preferable to living there. It is impossible to drive across town without spotting fluorescent arrows pointing the way to movie sets or construction sites plastered with handbills and posters announcing all manner of live spectacle, whether it be the Rolling Stones, *Phantom of the Opera* or WWF wrestling.

With a population of two million, Vancouver has entertainment venues that cater to all classes and demographics, ranging in style and capacity from the ornate and intimate to the sprawling and strictly functional. The city warrants a stop on every live performer's itinerary (despite the vagaries of the Canadian dollar), while its film industry—"Hollywood North"—attracts big-budget feature filmmakers. Not bad for a Wild West frontier town once solely inhabited by loggers, fishmongers, boatbuilders and assorted itinerant opportunists en route to or from the Klondike goldfields. From its earliest days, Vancouver possessed the potential to become a world-class city. By the end of the 19th century, that potential was already being realized.

As the late and legendary Vancouver saloon columnist Jack Wasserman once wrote, "By a process of attrition that knocked its competitors out of the race, Vancouver erupted as the café vaudeville capital of Canada, rivalling and finally outstripping Montreal in the east and San Francisco in the south as one of the few places where the brightest stars of the nightclub era could be glimpsed from behind a post, through a smoke-filled room, over the heads of the $20 tippers at ringside. Only in Las Vegas and Miami Beach, in season, were more superstars available in nightclubs."

Vancouver had been founded as a sawmill colony called Granville in 1870, the year before BC joined the Canadian Confederation. By the time the city was incorporated in 1886, the population was hovering around 1,000. That figure leaped the moment the Canadian Pacific Railway pulled into town on May 23, 1887, on the eve of Queen Victoria's Diamond Jubilee birthday. The port city had been, in theory at least, the last link in Her Royal Majesty's "glorious highway to India." Real estate speculation took off and British author Rudyard Kipling was among those who purchased investment property (even as newspapers warned of fraudulent real estate hawkers fleeing town for parts unknown). Teams of sled dogs bound for the Yukon were trained on city streets and plum seats at the Vancouver Opera House went to CPR bigwigs and the city's hookers, who occupied "a special place on the left-hand side under the boxes," according to promoter extraordinaire Ivan Ackery.

The Vancouver Opera House in 1898, located at 765 Granville Street. City of Vancouver Archives Bu P438

It all began when the Vancouver Opera House celebrated its grand opening February 9, 1891, with a performance of *Lohengrin* by the Emma Juch Grand Opera Company. The venue, financed by the CPR in exchange for real estate concessions, was constructed at 765 Granville, half a block from Robson Street and adjacent to the first Hotel Vancouver (which the CPR had opened four years earlier as part of the same deal). Despite a decade-long recession that began in the late 1880s and halted work on roads, bridges and railway lines, the Opera House sprang up and blossomed at a cost of $200,000 (about $5 million in today's dollars). It was an isle of opulence in an ocean of sawdust and mud.

Billed as "the showplace of the Pacific Northwest," the 1,200-seat Opera House was "the principal entertainment centre in the city," wrote Ackery in his 1980 autobiography *Fifty Years on Theatre Row*. "Streetcars used to line up to wait for the late theatre crowd, wreaking havoc with the traffic." Admission ranged from $1 for a seat in the gallery to $3 for an orchestra chair or $20 for a box capable of holding six (matinees were half-price). Power for electric lighting was pumped in from generators in the Hotel Vancouver next door, while a backup gaslight system was installed for emergencies. "The theatre was a place of plush and velvet, plaster cherubs and gargoyles," Ackery noted. "Patrons marvelled at its drop curtain, said to be one of the two finest in the world. It was an oil painting of the Three Sisters, Canmore's famous mountains, by a great artist. The work was unsigned but some thought it had been done by Lafayette. It took two flat cars to transport the curtain by rail from New York."

The cast of *Trial by Jury*, a popular production at the Vancouver Opera House in the early 1900s. City of Vancouver Archives Bu P397

Flashlight of Audiance Attending. Henry W. Savage's Production

The Vancouver Opera House had a capacity of 1,200. Ticket prices ranged from one to three dollars per person. City of Vancouver Archives Bu P389

The Vancouver Opera House played host to the biggest international stars and attractions of the vaudeville era: Sarah Bernhardt, Ethel Barrymore, The Boston Lyric Company, Blanche Walsh and Pollard's Lilliputian Opera Company from Australia. American author and humourist Mark Twain lectured at the venue. A production of *Ben Hur* boasted 275 actors and a live chariot race with each chariot harnessed to four horses running on treadmills. For obvious reasons, stagehands cleared the wings each night during this portion of the performance. Vaudeville, the single most popular form of entertainment in North America from 1875 to 1932, embraced any and all manner of performance, usually on the same night and on the same playbill. A typical show would include nine or 10 acts, though sometimes as many as 20.

The genre's snowballing success led to the formation of vaudeville circuits, as theatre chains set up shop in an ever-expanding network of cities and towns, each hiring a specific group of acts from the same booking agents. Notable were the Orpheum, Pantages and Paramount circuits, all of which extended to the Pacific Northwest. Over the years, star attractions would include George M. Cohan, Clifton Webb, Fay Templeton, Harry Houdini, Will Rogers, Nora Bayes, Ed Wynn, Bob Hope, Eddie Cantor, Fibber McGee and Molly, Jimmy Durante, Fred Allen, Jack Benny, George Burns and Gracie Allen, Sophie Tucker, Edgar Bergen, Tyrone Power, Douglas Fairbanks, Francis X. Bushman, W.C. Fields and Ethel Merman.

The Voice of Gold

By the time the Vancouver Opera House opened its doors in 1891, the city's population had boomed to 13,000 from 400 in a mere six years. With no other forum suitable for capitalizing on Vancouver's entertainment dollar, the Opera House was virtually guaranteed captive and sellout audiences. On September 21 of that year, "The Divine" Sarah Bernhardt starred in a production of *Fedora* at the venue. (She had stiff competition on opening night: a New Yorker named E.H. Hall was in town introducing Vancouverites to Thomas Edison's newfangled gramophone at the Manor House.)

Generally regarded as the greatest actress of the French theatre, Bernhardt was 47 at the time and had been a major international star since the 1870s. She toured Canada and the US nine times between 1880 and 1918 with her own independent troupe, performing solely in French and in venues ranging from grand and palatial theatre houses to dirt-floor tents and barns. Lauded for the emotional and graceful physical realism of her performances, Bernhardt wowed audiences with her rich and resonant *voix d'or* (voice of gold), noted for its clarity and bell-like tone. English biographer, critic and contemporary Lytton Strachey once observed, "In Sarah Bernhardt's voice there was more than gold: there was thunder and lightning; there was Heaven and Hell."

Although best known for her eccentricities (at 15, she purchased a coffin in which she sometimes slept), Bernhardt preferred more commonplace pursuits during her visits to Vancouver. In addition to her 1891 performance, she played the city again in 1913, one year before she lost her right leg in an accident at age 70. Regardless, she returned in 1918, performing onstage in a chair. "[She] was a good old soul, crazy about fishing," remembers stagehand W.H. "Buck" Taylor.

It was Taylor who carried Madame Bernhardt on and off the stage after she lost her leg, as well as in and out of fishing boats. The first major international star to appear in films, Bernhardt made a dozen of them, beginning with the French short *Le Duel d'Hamlet* in 1900. Although Bernhardt lent artistic credibility to the new medium, she remained skeptical of it until her death in 1923. Like vaudeville itself, she was a phenomenon of the stage.

Vaudeville hit its peak during the 1920s when an estimated 25,000 acts toured the continent at any given time, performing in over 4,000 venues for more than two million paying customers a day. The Vancouver Opera House, however, would not survive to see it. The CPR sold the theatre in 1911. The grand oil painting that had graced the drop curtain was subsequently defiled by hand-pasted playbills announcing newer, more colossal shows. Two years later, the structure was gutted by fire.

Above: Sarah Bernhardt unveiled her "voice of gold" in a production of *Fedora* at the Vancouver Opera House in 1891.
City of Vancouver Archives Port P1376
Left: Vancouver Public Library VPL 7333

Flickers

As the 20th century dawned, Vancouver's population more than doubled, reaching almost 30,000. Recessions and real estate windfalls came and went; St. Paul's Hospital, Woodward's department store and the University of British Columbia were built; and the first automobiles, airplanes and mailboxes arrived. Opium was outlawed and the Vancouver Stock Exchange incorporated. Meanwhile, an exhibition of Thomas Edison's primitive motion picture device, the Kinetoscope, had taken place at Market Hall in August 1897. The motion picture era had officially begun, forever altering the way human beings perceived and documented their existence.

On October 7, 1898, almost a decade to the day Edison filed his original patent for the Kinetoscope, 23-year-old Swedish-born entrepreneur John A. Schuberg opened Canada's first motion picture house in an empty storeroom on Cordova Street. Armed with a Kinetoscope and short streams of footage shot during the Spanish–American War earlier that year, Schuberg changed his name to Johnny Nash and gambled that films were more than a fad. Declining to join the hordes headed for the Klondike, he took his show on the road and struck gold at county fairs and carnivals on both sides of the Canada–US border. Curious onlookers filed into the promoter's 200-seat black tarpaulin tent to marvel at "flickers": short no-plot shots of nature, including a stirring 40-foot length of film called *A Rough Sea at Dover* that wowed viewers.

Although it would take 25 years, film would not only usurp vaudeville as the favoured form of North American family entertainment, it would render the latter redundant, cost-prohibitive and obsolete. Even though established vaudeville theatres were hesitant to transform into full-time film houses, the Nash, Pantages, and Sullivan and

Silent screen favourites Douglas Fairbanks and Mary Pickford on board the Chinese junk *Amoy*, which crossed the Pacific Ocean in 1922. City of Vancouver Archives Bu P134.3

Vaudeville houses such as the Pantages moved quickly to accommodate "flickers." Vancouver Public Library VPL S- 22311

Constantine circuits moved quickly to accommodate both forms of entertainment. Theatre owners, however, were so skeptical of the new medium that, when venues changed hands, a clause appeared on sales contracts obligating sellers to stay out of vaudeville if they planned on using the capital to open a movie house.

Frankenstein's Monster

Johnny Nash wasn't the only one staking his future on entertainment rather than mineral reserves. In 1909, a restless young Brit named Bill Pratt arrived in town after abandoning a family-funded education in diplomacy at King's College London. His family wasn't so enthused about his new path in theatre, so Pratt immigrated to Canada, supporting himself as a farmhand in Ontario, an actor in Kamloops, and a real estate agent, longshoreman and vaudeville stagehand in Vancouver. In 1910, he took a construction job working 10-hour days on the site of what would become the Pacific National Exhibition. Not surprisingly, the aspiring thespian wasn't entirely suited for, or smitten with, hoisting shovels and hammering nails.

Resolving to make it as an actor, Pratt changed his name to Boris Karloff. The first name, he felt, possessed dramatic appeal, while the Slavic surname derived from his mother's Russian ancestry. In an irony that can hardly be lost on those who've attended the garish annual attraction, Frankenstein's monster helped build the PNE. "Probably one of the greatest things that happened to me was in Vancouver," Karloff remarked in 1969, the same year he succumbed to a respiratory ailment at 81. "I was 22 years old. Someone offered me a half interest in a gold mine for £100. I had the money, too. I asked the advice of a banker friend and he said, 'No.' That mine was subsequently sold for £3 million. But imagine what would have happened to me. It would have ruined me."

Instead, Karloff embellished his résumé and scored a stage role in Seattle. Two decades later, he attained both stardom and immortality through his empathetic portrayal of the ghastly yet childlike creature in the 1931 film adaptation of Mary Shelley's *Frankenstein*. Although he uttered little more than a grunt and his eyes were obscured by mounds of makeup, Karloff instantly won over audiences, raised the standard for "horror films" (a term he disliked) and created one of the screen's earliest anti-heroes.

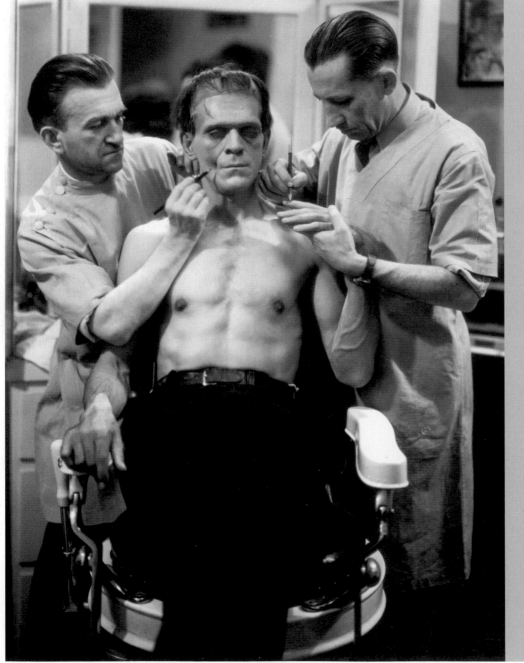

Struggling thespian Boris Karloff banged nails at the construction site of the PNE two decades before he achieved Hollywood immortality in the role of Frankenstein's monster.
MPTV.net

Queen of the Music Hall

Although most of the acts that ignited Vancouver stages in the early years flamed into obscurity almost immediately, the exceptions were notable. Already a star in England and South Africa by the time she arrived in North America, bawdy British singer and actress Marie Lloyd, "the Queen of the Music Hall," let her stiff upper lip get the better of her during her first visit to Vancouver. Happening upon a well-fed rat in the hallway outside her dressing room at the Opera House, she remarked to abashed handlers, "So, *this* is Canada."

Arriving in North America in 1913 for a six-month tour, Lloyd found herself embroiled in controversy and none too happy about it. The problems began when the married, 43-year-old performer disembarked in New York City with her boyfriend, Bernard Dillon, a washed-up and alcoholic Irish jockey 18 years

The cast of the *Gondoliers* onstage at the Vancouver Opera House at 765 Granville Street, April 1912. City of Vancouver Archives Bu P479.1

her junior. When a quayside immigration officer determined the pair were not married, Lloyd and Dillon were interned on Ellis Island, waiting to be deported back to England on grounds of "moral turpitude." Enraged and humiliated, the actress was informed on the morning of her impending departure that she and Dillon could remain temporarily—if they handed over £600 and stayed in separate hotels.

Marie Lloyd's temperament had not brightened a great deal by the time she and Dillon arrived in Vancouver a few weeks later. Her continent-wide reputation preceded her and a local licence inspector greeted the star with news that two numbers would be cut from her set, including a scandalous ditty entitled "The Ankle Watch," during which the singer lifted her dress and revealed—you guessed it—an ankle watch. Even with the censorship, concerned citizens lodged complaints and, by the end of Lloyd's week-long engagement at the New Orpheum, Vancouver mayor T.S. Baxter gave orders to stop the show. Stage manager Buck Taylor recalled, many years later, that he "battled in the wings with Miss Lloyd and some of her entourage after she had been refused permission to go onstage by the mayor. She sank her teeth into my chest!" Lily Laverock, the city's first female newspaper reporter (who became a successful entertainment promoter during the 1920s), claimed the brouhaha had little to do with Marie Lloyd—whom she described as a "kind-hearted and generous woman"—and all to do with the inebriated antics of Dillon. Whatever the case, Lloyd's cuckolded husband Alec Hurley died while she was abroad, allowing her and Dillon to wed in Portland, Oregon, in 1914. On the marriage certificate, the new Mrs. Dillon shaved seven years off her age.

It did little good. Finding herself in Canada once again in 1922, Lloyd had visibly deteriorated. Having adopted Dillon's drinking habits, she proved erratic and difficult to get onstage. She staggered about during a performance in Edmonton before collapsing altogether. The audience, thinking it part of the act, laughed uproariously. Lloyd was promptly returned to London, where she died shortly afterwards, at 52. Enthusiasts maintained that the spirit of the original British Music Hall died with her.

When not fighting in the wings with the tempestuous Marie Lloyd or carrying the elderly Sarah Bernhardt onto the stage, Buck Taylor had his work cut out for him. A local lad who, at age nine, began watching the door and running errands for performers at the Opera House shortly after its opening, Taylor adapted to theatre life at an early age. An integral part of his job entailed running next door to the Hotel Vancouver to procure crates of champagne for the acts. By the time he went to work at the New Orpheum, he was an old pro. Yet not even Taylor, as well-acquainted as he was with the eccentricities of stage performers, could have prepared himself for the Marx Brothers.

The vaudeville circuit brought the troupe to Vancouver in 1918 and again in 1922, seven years before the 1929 film *The Cocoanuts* catapulted them to silver-screen status. The clan proved as outrageous and chaotic offstage as on, Taylor discovered. After cajoling him into the New Orpheum's enormous backstage animal room, the brothers locked him in the lions' cage, all the while buckling over in laughter at his pronounced, and understandable, anxiety.

The Grand Old Lady

By the 1920s, Vancouver boasted 45 entertainment venues. While many clung to vaudeville, others were designed specifically for film. The Orpheum, Pantages, Imperial, Dominion, Rex, Empress, Strand, Royal, Globe, Maple Leaf, Columbia, Broadway, Capitol, Avenue and Colonial were but a handful of hotspots during Vancouver's "golden age" of theatre.

The greatest of Vancouver's entertainment centres was the Orpheum, though the name graced at least three different buildings prior to the 1927 opening of the existing structure at 884 Granville. The first, in the 900-block of Main Street (then called Westminster Avenue), began welcoming customers on October 3, 1904. Primarily a vaudeville house, it also showed "moving pictures" but ceased operation after only a few months. "That wasn't

Opposite: The second Orpheum Theatre opened its doors in 1906 at 805 W. Pender Street. City of Vancouver Archives Bu P440 N427

unusual at the time," says Vancouver writer John Mackie, co-author of *Vancouver: The Unknown City*. "Many of those early theatres were just tiny rooms in converted retail spaces. They were converted into theatres by installing a few rows of benches and a stage or a screen. Admission was usually five cents; hence the name 'nickelodeons.'"

The second Orpheum opened December 17, 1906, in the former People's Theatre at the northwest corner of Pender and Howe. "Carl Berch, the owner of People's Theatre, didn't take kindly to being evicted so someone else could take over," says Mackie. "So he locked himself inside with 10 employees and a cache of guns. The dispute boiled to a head when a group of 30 men hired by the new owners attempted to sneak in through an upstairs window in the wee small hours of the morning. Berch fired three shots into the dark but, luckily, no one was hit. He and his employees were overwhelmed pretty quickly and evicted on the spot." Today the 1,200-seat hall is remembered mostly for Charlie Chaplin's appearance there with Karno's Comedians in 1912 and for its unusual design. "It looked like a barn," says Mackie.

The third Orpheum, at the former site of the Vancouver Opera House on Granville near Robson, opened March 17, 1913, and played host to the likes of Sarah Bernhardt, the Marx Brothers, Harry Houdini, Jack Benny, Fred Astaire, Bob Hope and Gracie Allen. Later converted into a movie house, it became the Vancouver Theatre in 1927, the Lyric in 1935 and the International Cinema in 1947. Despite being one of Vancouver's oldest buildings, erected in 1891, it was demolished in 1969 during the construction of the Pacific Centre Mall.

The fourth Orpheum, which is still with us today, took 800 workers 10 months to complete. The 3,000-seat room cost $1.25 million and opened November 7, 1927 (the same year Al Jolson's "talkie," *The Jazz Singer*, forever changed the playing field for motion pictures). Designed in the Spanish Renaissance style by Glasgow-born architect B. Marcus Priteca (responsible for creating more than 100 entertainment venues, including the Paramount in

Above: Performers onstage at the Orpheum. City of Vancouver Archives CVA 470-22

Opposite: Illusionist Harry Houdini captivated the city when he hung from the *Vancouver Sun* building to advertise a new Orpheum show. City of Vancouver Archives Port N100

A crowd gathers at the Orpheum box office to buy tickets for the 1946 movie *Lady Luck*.
City of Vancouver Archives CVA 1184-2306

Seattle and the Pantages theatres in Hollywood and Vancouver), it epitomized the ideal of the early 20th century movie palace. Silk tapestries adorned wall panels and $100,000 of gold leaf was applied to ceilings, columns and archways. A hand-painted dome and gleaming chandeliers lent the interior a baroque look, while the foyer was modelled after an East Indian temple. The orchestra pit held 20 musicians and an enormous Wurlitzer organ, its ascending pipes concealed behind screens on either side of the sprawling stage. When builder Joseph Francis Langer tried to save money by cancelling delivery of the $45,000 instrument, the Cincinnati-based Wurlitzer company threatened to sue.

According to retired UBC theatre professor Norman Young, also the former head of the Civic Theatres Board that maintains the Orpheum, "You escaped your drab little life by coming into this make-believe place, a picture palace." The first playbill included vaudeville acts Jack "King of the Kazoo" Howe and Toto the Beloved Clown, tango dancers Chaney and Fox, as well as "photoplay," featuring *The Wise Wife* with silent-screen star Phyllis Haver. Entertainment lineups changed weekly, with singer-songwriter Gene Austin headlining shortly after it opened, cresting on the wave of his hit, "My Blue Heaven." The first talking motion picture to play the theatre was 1928's *The Leatherneck* starring William Boyd, who would go on to portray Hopalong Cassidy in 66 films between 1935 and 1948.

As many entertainment houses were part of larger, US-based chains, theatre managers were often American. It

didn't take their Canadian cousins long, however, to learn the ropes. A new breed of showbiz professional—not actor, agent or promoter but a canny combination of all three—had been spawned: the impresario. In Vancouver, the names Ivan Ackery and Hugh Pickett would become synonymous with the term. It wasn't the type of career you studied for in school and it wasn't hard to separate the bandwagon jumpers from the real deal. Although a fine eye for talent, a sharp mind for business and an almost clairvoyant sense of what the public wanted to see and hear were essential for success in the business, impresarios were, above all else, fans.

The World's Greatest Showman

Born in 1899 in Bristol, England, Ivan Ackery was dispatched to military school at an early age, after his widowed mother immigrated to North America. Following her to Vancouver in 1914, he bounced around western Canada doing odd jobs before landing a $5-a-week post as an usher at Calgary's opulent Capitol Theatre in 1921. Returning to the West Coast in 1923, Ackery scored a job at Vancouver's Capitol on Granville Street, built in 1921 and capable of holding 2,100 patrons.

"[In 1923], the uppermost thought in my mind was to get into the theatre business," he later recalled. "That's exactly what I did and I worked night shift for the next 50 years! For me it was a joy. I loved meeting the public and

Louis Armstrong was one visiting performer that local impresario and madcap promoter Ivan Ackery had no hope of upstaging.
Vancouver Sun

Opposite: Ever the charmer, Orpheum Theatre manager Ivan Ackery greets Marilyn Monroe during her publicity tour for *Gentlemen Prefer Blondes.* Vancouver Public Library VPL 59307 *The Province*

Santa Claus was a relatively minor celebrity in the rolodex of Orpheum manager Ivan Ackery (right). City of Vancouver Archives CVA 1184-2229

I loved the films. Something new was happening every few days, films changing, different promotions happening, and that—the promotion—was the part of the business I came to love the best. I learned as I went along."

He was well-schooled, having worked at Vancouver's Capitol from 1922 to 1928, the Victoria Road Theatre from 1928 to 1930, the Dominion from 1930 to 1931, Victoria's Capitol in 1932, Vancouver's Royal in 1933, the Strand in 1934 and, most famously, the Orpheum Theatre from 1935 to 1969. Ackery plied his trade with flash and pizzazz, often upstaging the evening's entertainment. The Atomic Ack, as he was known, sang in the aisles, tap danced onstage, beat drums on street corners, stuck his head in trick guillotines and performed with his sidekick, Bambi the Singing Dog.

His promotional campaigns were equally over the top. Ushers and usherettes were decked out as cowboys, pirates and Ziegfeld showgirls. Whatever the theme of the show, Ackery cooked up a zany scheme to plug it. Unlike today, when first-run movies open on dozens of multiplex screens simultaneously, the gilded cinemas on Granville's luminescent Theatre Row competed for premieres and Ackery usually landed the big ones. Airplanes flew banners across the city heralding upcoming attractions, kids were crowned kings and queens at weekend matinees and even Burrard Band Native leader Chief Dan George was roped into Ackery's service, appearing at the Orpheum in traditional tribal garb to promote director John Ford's 1964 Western *Cheyenne Autumn* (never mind that the chief wasn't a Cheyenne).

Ackery, a two-time winner of the Quigley Award for Best Theatre Manager in North America, proved as adept at handling temperamental celebrities as drumming up wild promotions. For the February 16, 1940, premiere of *Gone With the Wind*, he cabled Vivien Leigh (who played Scarlett O'Hara) to ask if her six-year-old daughter Suzanne, enrolled at a Vancouver boarding school, could attend opening night. Leigh consented on the condition that the press not be notified, much to Ackery's disappointment. Two years later, he carried Susan Hayward onstage after she sprained her ankle at the world premiere of *The Forest Rangers*. A decade after that, he was photographed on the arm of Marilyn Monroe during the blonde bombshell's 1953 visit promoting *Gentlemen Prefer Blondes*.

Granville Street looks radically different today than it did in 1946, but the Orpheum and the Commodore remain.
City of Vancouver Archives CVA 1184-2290

Drinking buddies with Gary Cooper (star of 1952's *High Noon*), the pair once accompanied Vancouver mayor Fred Hume to a bootlegger's den, where they became well lubricated before returning to the Orpheum. After introducing Cooper to the audience, Ackery returned to the wings to find Cooper convulsing with laughter, gleefully waiting to inform Ack that his fly had been open the entire time. By 4:30 the following morning, Cooper was still at it, dancing with the cleaning lady. When he finally stumbled into Granville Street, he hitched a ride to the Hotel Vancouver on an early morning street-cleaning vehicle. "Coop got me into lots of trouble," Ackery said. A photograph of the pair in the mid-1950s shows a visibly besotted Cooper, aged well beyond his years. Cooper died of lung cancer in 1962, less than a week after his 60th birthday. Ackery passed away in 1989, at 90. In addition to making Vancouver's Orpheum what it was, he and Hugh Pickett were instrumental in making it what it would become, spearheading a 1973 drive to save the "Grand Old Lady of Granville" from demolition.

Notably, the Commodore Ballroom opened two years after and a few doors down from the Orpheum, at 868 Granville Street, on December 3, 1929. Built by booze baron George Conrad Reifel and designed by architect

H.H. Gillingham, the second-storey art-deco dance hall featured an expansive New York-style stage suitable for big bands and a remarkable sprung dance floor: a hardwood surface that literally bounced and undulated beneath dancers' feet thanks to an underlying layer of horsehair stretched across a bed of rubber tires. Forced to close four months later due to the stock market crash the previous fall, the Commodore was reopened in November 1930 by Nick Kogas and Johnny Dillias. The dinner-and-dance club built a strong following over the years and was taken over in 1961 by Reifel's nephew Dick Gourlay.

At the same time as the Orpheum faced demolition in the early 1970s, the Commodore was busy reinventing itself. Starting in 1970, promoter Drew Burns transformed the Commodore into one of the hottest entertainment venues in North America. Capable of holding in excess of 1,000 patrons (in excess being the rule rather than the exception), the room hosted hundreds of top-ranked international performers over the ensuing quarter-century, including Dizzy Gillespie, Tina Turner, Marianne Faithful, Iggy Pop, KISS, David Bowie, Emmylou Harris, the Police, the Clash, U2, R.E.M., the Pixies, Nirvana and Pearl Jam, not to mention scores of Vancouver-based acts. Shortly after Burns's lease expired in 1995, however, the venue closed its doors. In a replay of the "Save the Orpheum" campaign, House of Blues Concerts, rock manager Bruce Allen and businessman Roger Gibson came to the rescue, investing $3.5 million to restore and renovate the room. The Commodore Ballroom reopened on November 12, 1999.

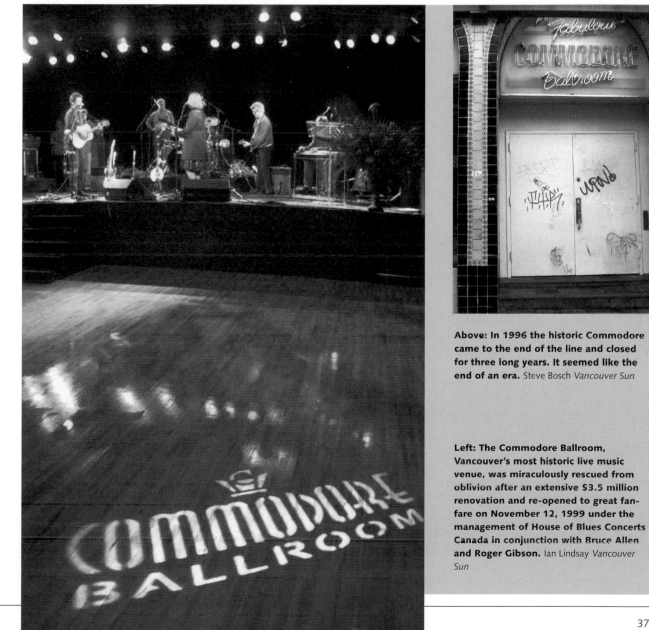

Above: In 1996 the historic Commodore came to the end of the line and closed for three long years. It seemed like the end of an era. Steve Bosch *Vancouver Sun*

Left: The Commodore Ballroom, Vancouver's most historic live music venue, was miraculously rescued from oblivion after an extensive $3.5 million renovation and re-opened to great fan-fare on November 12, 1999 under the management of House of Blues Concerts Canada in conjunction with Bruce Allen and Roger Gibson. Ian Lindsay *Vancouver Sun*

Vancouverite Sadie Marks (aka Mary Livingstone) met her future husband Jack Benny during one of his stopovers in the city. City of Vancouver Archives CVA 1184-524

Below: the Jack Benny troupe: Marks, Benny, Phil Harris, Don Wilson and Eddie Anderson (seated). City of Vancouver Archives CVA 1184-517

Stage Door Janie

Seattle-born Sadie Marks had no intention of becoming an entertainer. In fact, the girl disliked and distrusted showbiz types intensely. By 1922, when Sadie was 14, her father had relocated the family to Vancouver where the elder Marks, a prominent businessman, had invited some out-of-town relatives to the family home at 1649 Nelson Street to observe Passover. Only one of them, Zeppo Marx, showed up, dragging in tow Jack Benny, the comedian and musician opening for the Marx Brothers at the New Orpheum. Benny, whom Zeppo had lured to the Marks's household under the pretense of attending a wild party, did little to sway young Sadie's opinion of "hoofers and crooners." When the girl, at her parents' behest, broke out a violin and began sawing away at it, Benny visibly cringed, moaning to Zeppo in an unintentional stage whisper, "Let's get outta here."

For Sadie, later known to radio and television audiences as Mary Livingstone and to a coterie of subservient underlings as "Mrs. Jack Benny," it was an inauspicious debut. The humiliation was repaid in kind, however, when the girl and some pals from King George High School took in one of Benny's performances at the New Orpheum a few days later. Planting themselves in the front row, the girls mercilessly heckled the 28-year-old entertainer for the duration of his show. Later Sadie's family moved

Phil Harris, Jack Benny's band leader, signs autographs at a live broadcast from the Forum in 1944. City of Vancouver Archives CVA 1184-529

back to the San Francisco Bay area and when she tried to reintroduce herself backstage at one of Benny's shows, he dismissed her as one more Stage Door Janie. But fate kept thrusting the two together. They began dating and eventually Benny proposed.

Jack Benny and Sadie Marks wed January 14, 1927, at the Clayton Hotel in Waukegan, Illinois, in an Orthodox Jewish ceremony. Sadie fainted at the end of the ceremony when Jack stomped on the glass. Not long after, Sadie asked Jack if he remembered a Passover supper he had attended in Vancouver with Zeppo Marx five years earlier. "I'll never forget," Benny said. "There was a silly little girl all dressed up in her sister's clothes." Sadie replied, "You married her."

Benny, who had joked onstage for years about his "dumb girlfriend," enlisted such a character into his act shortly after his marriage. When the actress hired to play the role, Marie Marsh, unexpectedly took ill, Jack asked Sadie to step in for the West Coast leg of the tour. Garnering rave reviews and overwhelming audience approval, the show hit the Los Angeles Orpheum only to have Marsh return with less-than-satisfactory results. Following the first night's performance, the theatre manager took Benny aside and demanded to know how such a dreadful actress had won thumbs-up accolades the previous week. "That was no actress," Benny replied, echoing a well-worn one-liner, "that was my wife." The manager insisted that Sadie, brandishing her new stage name, Mary Livingstone, be reinstated. The professional union lasted, on stage, radio and television, until her retirement from show business in 1958. The personal union lasted until Benny's death from pancreatic cancer on December 26, 1974, at 80.

"Oh, Jack was wonderful," says Vancouver impresario Hugh Pickett. "Jack was always wonderful. He had different girl singers with him each time and would always give them a good hunk of the stage. He treated them like human beings rather than nothings, which is how a lot of those people treated their singers. Mary Livingstone, on the other hand, was a ... Oh, God, she was awful. It was like she hated everybody. She demanded to be addressed as 'Mrs. Jack Benny.' She'd say, 'Don't ever tell me to do something I don't want to do,' so I'd have to go up to her and say, 'Mary, do you think we should ... blah, blah, blah?' It was so stupid. And she was from Vancouver, after all. Her only claim to fame was having sold stockings in LA."

BACKSTAGE VANCOUVER

By 1930, silent movies were dead and vaudeville was being hoofed out the backstage door. The 1929 stock market crash and ensuing depression hit North America hard, but as Hugh Pickett has noted, in some ways it was the best thing that ever happened to the entertainment industry. People desperately needed escape and an afternoon concert or an evening at the movies unburdened them, however temporarily, of their woes.

Talking motion pictures arrived in Vancouver in 1928, and by early 1929 colour movies were being exhibited at the Granville Street Kodak store. In 1932, celebrated pianist and composer (and later Polish prime minister) Ignacy Paderewski gave a recital at the Vancouver Arena. The Vancouver Folk Festival (then called the Vancouver Folksong and Dance Festival) kicked off in 1933 and the Vancouver Symphony Orchestra gave its first concert at Stanley Park's Malkin Bowl in 1934. The following year, the Kitsilano Showboat began holding amateur talent contests during the summer. The city was on the verge of an era, Pickett says, "when there were nearly more stages in town than talent to fill them."

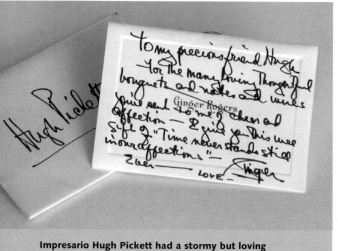

Impresario Hugh Pickett had a stormy but loving relationship with song-and-dance queen Ginger Rogers.
Hugh Pickett Collection

The foundations of BC's film industry were laid in 1927 when the British Parliament passed the British Cinematograph Film Act. In an attempt to restrict the flow of American-made films into British theatres, UK exhibitors were obliged to run a hefty quota of British-made productions. Wily producers and directors in the New World, however, immediately spotted a lucrative loophole: the act recognized films produced in any of the Commonwealth countries as being "British." Hollywood moguls, therefore, dispatched a hard-working handful of hacks to Victoria, where they set up studios overnight and commenced grinding out slapdash products suitable for meeting the quota requirements, which resulted in the genre's nickname: Quota Quickies.

Stanley Park's open air theatre Malkin Bowl became the home of pioneer repertory company Theatre Under the Stars in 1940. City of Vancouver Archives CVA 1184-1963

In 1935 alone, several dozen quota films were fired off before authorities clued in and blocked distribution of the bogus "British" movies. Although they were generally dismissed as "less than B-grade" by film historians, at least one rising star, Rita Hayworth, appeared in two of them: *Across the Border* and *Convicted*, both filmed in Victoria and released in 1937.

The Impresario

On November 12, 1927, a few days after the Orpheum's inauguration, 14-year-old Hugh Pickett ventured to the downtown theatre and saw his first motion picture. It marked the beginning of a lifelong passion. "In 1929, I lied about my age and went to work at the Colonial Theatre at Granville and Dunsmuir," remembers Pickett. "I was 16 but I told them I was 18."

Struggling through McGee High, Pickett was relieved to escape the drudgery of school for a world more suited to his gregarious nature (his mother and father had met at the old Opera House). "I was an usher, a doorman, a sweeper. I did everything," he says. "My first job was to go into a room in a basement that had been condemned because it was full of old advertising papers for the movies, mostly silent ones. I took barrels of this stuff into the alley and burned it. It took almost three weeks. In those days, I just thought, 'Gloria Swanson, who's she? Charlie Chaplin, who cares? Mary Pickford, burn her!'

The Colonial was one of Vancouver's original movie theatres.
Vancouver Public Library VPL 11025

Impresario *supremo* Hugh Pickett accompanied by followers of fine fashion at the opening of the Vogue Theatre in 1941.

Can you imagine what all of those things would be worth today? At the time, of course, I had no thought of the historical value."

Pickett's sense of values would soon change. Working in the Colonial from 11 a.m. to 11 p.m. daily for $7.50 a week, he commuted via interurban streetcars or, if he missed the last one of the evening, walked home from downtown to Kerrisdale. "With the kind of money I was making in those days, you didn't call a cab," he says. "Sometimes you'd get a ride with somebody. You didn't worry about getting picked up because—again, in those days—you knew they weren't going to do anything other than drive you where you wanted to go."

Pickett worked three summers at the Colonial, right into the Depression. "The Depression was the best thing that ever happened to entertainment, because if you wanted to get the hell away from your problems, that was how you did it. The Colonial was cheap: 10 cents in the daytime, 25 cents at night for adults and 10 cents for kids. It did a good business." Flamboyant mayor L.D. Taylor was one of Pickett's regular visitors. "He lived in an

THE ORPHEUM

B | 32 | 7

SOUND
AND
VISION

CHAPTER TWO

A
BACKSTAGE
VANCOUVER
PRODUCTION

SEPTEMBER 21
7:30 PM

Patrons are required to abide by the
Terms & Conditions outlined on the
reverse of this ticket

B ADMIT
ONE

VANCOUVER
CITY
CENTRE

NO ADMITTANCE
AFTER CURTAIN RAISED
NO EXCEPTIONS

apartment at Robson and Granville," recounts Pickett, "and he always walked up and down Granville Street wearing his trademark red scarf and talking to everybody. He always came into the Colonial and talked to me, though he never looked at a movie. He was probably the most famous mayor the town ever had."

Leaving both the theatre and high school in 1931, Pickett went to work first for the Port Warden's office, where he typed and took shorthand ("I got an award in high school as the fastest typist in Canada," he says), and later at his father Fred's steamship company, Dingwall Cotts. It was through this connection that young Hugh met his first celebrity, Oscar-nominated actor Lewis Stone. Probably best remembered as Judge James K. Hardy, father to Mickey Rooney's Andy Hardy in the 1937 to 1947 film series, Stone had received an Academy Award nomination for playing the treacherous Count Pahlen in 1928's *The Patriot*. Having navigated his luxury yacht from Los Angeles to Alaska, Stone laid over in Vancouver, where Pickett's father assisted him servicing the vessel. "Mr. Stone asked us all to dinner on the boat and my mother and father and I went," says Pickett, noting that he himself was a "real smartass at 19 and thought I knew more about movies than he did." Stone's yacht was in town for four days, and on the third day, the actor asked the star-struck kid if he would like to join the party for the cruise back to Long Beach, California. "Mr. Stone said, 'You can take the train from Long Beach into Hollywood and I'll give you my secretary's name and she can show you the ropes.' I thought, 'My God, Heaven has opened its gates!'"

Feeling like a king, Pickett set sail for Los Angeles, where Stone secured him a suite at the Hollywood Plaza Hotel on Hollywood Boulevard. Invited to dine with Stone's secretary at the Brown Derby ("I knew from reading movie magazines that it was the place to go"), he was introduced to scriptwriter and RKO assistant Lela Rogers. After dinner, the trio visited RKO Studios and hooked up with Lela's daughter, Ginger. "She'd made only one big movie at the time and I'd happened to see it," says Pickett of Ginger Rogers. "I thought she was wonderful." The pair remained lifelong friends and Rogers often visited Pickett at his Vancouver home, poring over movie stills and

Hugh Pickett enjoys a chuckle with Ginger Rogers (above) and a howl with Mitzi Gaynor (right).
Hugh Pickett Collection *Vancouver Sun*

Pickett in 1977. Reflecting on his role in Vancouver entertainment, he said, "I loved doing it and I didn't give a damn about the money." *Vancouver Sun*

preparing dinners in Pickett's kitchen. "She made herself at home here and she was a good cook," he says.

At 20, Pickett inherited "a pile of money" from an aunt who'd been married to a wealthy hotelier. He set sail from New York on the luxury liner *Normandie* and spent two years touring the world first-class. He joined the army during World War II and served four years as a typist and stenographer to a brigadier general stationed in an office at the old Hotel Vancouver at Georgia and Granville. A plum part of his duties entailed escorting movie stars around town during celebrity fundraisers for the war effort, among them Susan Hayward and Jack Benny. "I'd pick them up at the airport with the brigadier's car and chauffeur and we'd take them to the corner of Granville and Hastings, where they'd do a spiel to collect money, then we'd go over to the Orpheum Theatre for a benefit that night." The serendipity of the situation was not lost on Pickett: "For me, it was a strange war. It had nothing to do with war, for God's sake. It mostly had to do with typing."

After the war, Pickett went to work for friend and talent-booker Gordon Hilker. When Hilker went bankrupt in 1949 and relocated to Toronto to start over, Pickett and Hilker's former secretary, Holly Maxwell, picked up

the ball, becoming Vancouver's promoters for prominent New York agent Sol Hurok. "He was the greatest purveyor of talent in America," says Pickett, "and he went almost hysterical when Gordon declared bankruptcy because a lot of his acts were under contract to Hilker. So he flew out from New York and said, 'Are you guys still going? You can't quit now. You gotta go on!' He handled all of the world's great artists out of New York. He didn't like anybody, but for some reason, he liked me. He was like a god to me. He knew what he was doing."

Becoming both a friend and mentor, Hurok inspired Pickett to found Famous Artists Ltd. "We ran a very loose business, with five employees," he says. "I remember one time when we hired a new girl. She was at the ticket wicket and a woman came up quite late, just as the concert was beginning, and said, 'One, please.' The girl at the wicket said, 'That'll be $7.50.' Well, rather indignantly the woman replied, '$7.50 *apiece*?' The girl shot back, 'Honey, a ticket is $7.50. A *piece* will cost you $50.' And the woman stomped away. This was the girl's first night. I said, 'You're in, baby. You're in!' We laughed about that one for years."

Although Holly Maxwell would leave the fold upon finding a husband, Pickett went on to book virtually every major act to appear in Vancouver between the 1940s and mid-1980s, including Jack Benny, Bob Hope, Louis Armstrong, Marlene Dietrich, Igor Stravinsky, Nat King Cole, Katharine Hepburn, Arthur Rubenstein, Rudolf Nureyev, Phyllis Diller, Elvis Presley, Bette Midler, Sir Laurence Olivier and the Rolling Stones. "It was a lot of work," says Pickett, who received the Order of Canada in 1987 and retired from show business 11 years later at 85. "It was a lot harder work than I'd ever thought of doing. But it didn't matter how late it went or how much trouble it was. I loved doing it and I didn't give a damn about the money."

Leading Ladies

As the film industry pushed forward, many a silent film star was left on the cutting-room floor. Some simply lacked sufficient talent and training to perform in sound pictures; others, including Lillian Gish, scorned and resisted them on principle, believing silent films had a greater impact on audiences. Despite an astounding career that took off in 1912 when she met groundbreaking director D. W. Griffith (who cast her in more than 40 films, including 1915's *The Birth of a Nation* and 1916's *Intolerance*), Gish was dropped by MGM in 1928. The "First Lady of the Silent Screen" returned to the stage and stayed there for the next half century. In the 1940s, however, she recanted her initial dismissal of sound films and made a clutch of them, including 1946's *Duel in the Sun*, for which she received an Academy Award nomination for Best Supporting Actress.

"Lillian Gish was quite a lady and I knew her very well," says Pickett, who befriended the actress decades after her star had faded. "She always said, 'Mary [Pickford] did it first,' though, in fact, Lillian was in silent movies before Mary. They were great friends. Lillian was the smartest cookie in the business. She owned the building she lived in on 57th Street in New York and rented every apartment to somebody in the movie business. We had her at the Orpheum twice in the sixties and did good business. We ran some of her silent movies; then she talked about movies and her parts. People asked questions. I thought I'd lose money but, in fact, I made money. She was brilliant—quick, quick, quick—I just loved her. She died in her own bed in 1993, at 99, six months before her 100th birthday."

Gish had been pals with Joan Crawford, whom she met when the latter signed on as a contract player at MGM in 1925, at 21. Four years later, Crawford married her first of five husbands, Douglas Fairbanks Jr., securing a place in Hollywood's royal circle. Gifted with a powerful speaking voice and a talent that equalled her ambition, Crawford moved flawlessly into sound pictures, though she trampled over countless rivals along the way. A backlash was inevitable. Labelled "box office poison" by an industry trade paper in 1938, her career nose-dived and MGM head Louis B. Mayer saw to it that she received increasingly insubstantial roles before dropping her altogether in 1943. "Joan was under contract to MGM for 18 years and she couldn't believe it when they dumped her," says Pickett. "Two years later, she got a contract from Warner Brothers to do *Mildred Pierce* and won the Academy Award for Best

**Hollywood pioneer Lillian Gish provided Vancouver fans
with a memorable account of her career in silent film.**
City of Vancouver Archives CVA 1184-400

THE ORPHEUM

B | 32 | 7

CHAPTER TWO

SOUND AND VISION

A BACKSTAGE VANCOUVER PRODUCTION

SEPTEMBER 21 7:30 PM

Patrons are required to abide by the terms & conditions outlined on the reverse of this ticket.

B ADMIT ONE

VANCOUVER CITY CENTRE

NO ADMITTANCE AFTER CURTAIN RAISED

NO EXCEPTIONS

Actress. It was the biggest laugh; everybody had hysterics."

In 1959, Crawford's fifth and final husband, Pepsi-Cola chairman Alfred Nu Steele, passed away and Crawford inherited both his millions and a seat on Pepsi's board of directors. In addition to having made a substantial fortune in film, she had married well, several times. "Joan was living in an elegant New York apartment," says Pickett, "and she had tons of money. She was a tough cookie but she was a smart cookie. I liked her. Then, a year after her death [in 1977], all these weird stories starting coming out of the woodwork."

A scathing indictment by adopted daughter Christina Crawford, *Mommie Dearest*, was published in 1978 and filmed in 1981 with Faye Dunaway portraying Crawford. "That was just terrible," says Pickett. "Her friends would say, 'Well, she asked for it. She just had to have two children, so she adopted two children that had absolutely nothing to do with each other.' Those children hated each other and they hated her. I never did find out what happened to those kids. They were adults and still living with her."

Whatever the grounds for the unflattering accusations, Gish confided to Pickett that there was a side to her friend that the public simply didn't know. "Lillian went to lunch at Joan's New York apartment one day in the late 1960s," he says, "and there was a noise coming from the kitchen. Joan said, 'Oh, I'm making lunch because the housekeeper isn't here today.' But Lillian knew there was somebody in the kitchen and finally asked, 'Who's that?' Joan said, 'Well, I didn't want to tell you but it's Franchot.' It was Franchot Tone." Tone, a suave but hopelessly B-grade actor throughout the thirties, forties and fifties, had been Crawford's second husband from 1935 to 1939. Three decades later, he was dying of lung cancer and Crawford made a point of caring for him. "He was a lonely man, by that time," says Pickett. "He was sick and in a wheelchair. Joan would have him over a couple of times a week and make him lunch. It gave him something to do.

"Lillian told me once, 'You know, I shudder to think about it but everybody thought Joan was so tough, that she wouldn't do anything for anybody. But she wasn't tough at all.' Here she was, looking after this man whom she hasn't even seen for years since they'd been divorced and he was welcome at her apartment at all times. Joan wasn't that bad."

Neither was Ginger Rogers, with whom Pickett maintained a lifelong friendship after meeting the budding star in Los Angeles in 1932, the year before she became one of Hollywood's biggest box office stars and top moneymakers. Her big break came when she nabbed a starring role in 1933's *Professional Sweetheart*, followed by prestigious supporting roles in *42nd Street* and *Gold Diggers of 1933* (which introduced the musical standard "We're in the Money"). That same year, she teamed with dancer and actor Fred Astaire for the first time, in *Flying Down to Rio*. The pair churned out a series of extravagant musicals featuring songs by the likes of George and Ira Gershwin, Cole Porter and Irving

Ginger Rogers making backstage preparations at the Cave. David Boswell

Berlin. "Fred and Ginger worked together as partners for over a decade but never once set foot in each other's home," says Pickett. "Theirs was a completely professional relationship."

By the 1950s, Rogers's shining light had been eclipsed by a new breed of Hollywood sweetheart (notably Marilyn Monroe) and the actress returned primarily to stage work. In 1965, however, any doubts about her enduring star status were swiftly squelched when she took the lead in the smash Broadway musical, *Hello, Dolly!* "The show came to Vancouver with Ginger for a one-week run," Pickett recalls, "and Ginger's mother Lela came up from Los Angeles to see her. I set her up with two seats at the theatre and then she came backstage. That's when

she opened her purse to dig out a pack of cigarettes." Ginger, a devout Christian Scientist, went berserk.

"I was with Ginger on the other side of the stage, preparing to take her to her dressing room," says Pickett. "But when she saw her mother tapping the cigarette on the package, she just blew. She screamed at her mother across the stage, then went over and lambasted her in front of the stage crew: 'You're in error!' she screamed. Being 'in error' is a big crime in Christian Science. I ran across the stage and said, 'Ginger, *you're* in error. Come to your dressing room.'" Pickett admonished Rogers: "'How can you talk to your mother like that and have everybody in the theatre hate you? Yet you're full of God and religion?'" Rogers' response was to cancel the evening's plans and not phone Pickett until more than a week later, once she'd returned home to Palm Springs. "I said, 'Well, have you straightened Lela out?' She said, 'That was kind of stupid of me, wasn't it?' Ginger made more than 85 films and a lot of money and it all went to the Christian Science Church." Rogers spent a great deal of time in Vancouver and performed at the Cave Supper Club on Hornby Street twice in the 1970s, selling out both performances in short order. "She was quite a gal," says Pickett. "I saw her three weeks before she died [in 1995, at 83]. I went down to Seattle and had lunch with her. By then, she was in a wheelchair. I didn't dare say, 'If you believe in Christian Science to such an extent, why are you in a wheelchair?'"

According to author and retired *Vancouver Sun* columnist Denny Boyd, Pickett knew how to reward his standout performers. When a Soviet ballet company did extraordinarily well in town, "Hughie was delighted," says Boyd. "Realizing the way things were in what was then the USSR, he was in the lobby of the Hotel Georgia passing out money to these people, just little cash bonuses to show his extreme gratitude because they had gone a step beyond. Well, Hughie gave one of the women, a Russian ballerina, $25 and said to her, 'Why don't you go up to the store here (Eaton's on Georgia Street) and buy something for yourself?' Hugh didn't think much more of it until he heard this amazing clatter out in front of the hotel, on the sidewalk. Here comes this ballerina and she's pushing a manual lawnmower."

Leading Men

As well as the ladies, there were the gents. Pickett brought the greatest actors, musicians and performers of the 20th century to Vancouver, including Sir John Gielgud, Sir Laurence Olivier, Jack Benny, Bob Hope, Elvis Presley, Harry Belafonte, Fred Astaire, Benny Goodman, Victor Borge, Rudolf Nureyev, Marcel Marceau, Liberace, Igor Stravinsky and Arthur Rubenstein.

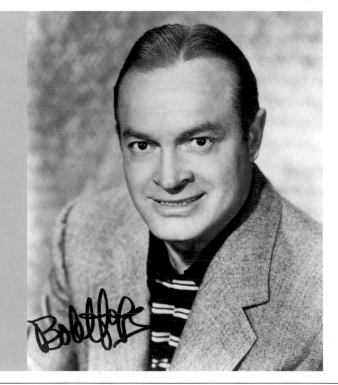

Bob Hope came to know more about the city than many of its inhabitants.
BC Entertainment Hall of Fame

Opposite: Ginger Rogers performing with Sid Caesar in *Anything Goes*, August 27, 1980. Colin Price *The Province*

Below: Pickett admires Sir Laurence Olivier's latest necktie. Dame Jane Edgeworth (centre). Hugh Pickett Collection

Above: Hugh Pickett, as always, at Bob Hope's left side. Hugh Pickett Collection

"Bob Hope was a good friend from way back in the thirties, when he was doing his first radio show," says Pickett. "I knew the woman who was the producer of the show and I met him when I was 19 years old. Bob came here all the time and always asked for me to be there and sit on his left-hand side because he could only hear out of that one ear. He'd say, 'Hughie always sits on my left side because he knows I can't hear out of my right ear. This way, I can hear what he's saying and I can talk to him. Besides, he's the only one in the room who knows what I'm talking about.' And it was true! He'd be talking about something that happened in the forties, during *his* forties, and nobody else in the room had even been born then."

An equally solid friendship developed with Sir Laurence Olivier, largely over a matter of neckties. When the British stage great arrived for a 1967 Canadian tour with London's National Theatre Company, Pickett was asked to accompany the troupe on the road. "I became good friends with him on the first day," says Pickett of Olivier. "He asked me to do something with the stage. I had it done and it impressed him. I ended up on the tour with him for six weeks and we had a ball. He insisted I call him 'Larry.'

"The second day he was here, he said to me, 'Oh, I have such terrible ties. They're all English and they're just awful. But your ties are so great.' I said, 'Okay, here,' and I took off my tie and gave it to him. Then he said, 'Hmm, it doesn't quite look the same, does it?' So I said, 'Okay, wait until I get a better tie.' The next day, I brought him a new tie and he said, 'Now, *that's* a better tie!' And from that day on, he got ties right across Canada. I told him, 'Look, I'm looking after you. So let me look after you. Don't try and do things you don't think you want to do; let me do them.' So we really bonded. When it was all over and he was back in England and I was back in Vancouver, he'd phone and say something silly, just to be funny. He was a good man."

Russian-born ballet dancer Rudolf Nureyev, on the other hand, could be downright malevolent. His limber years behind him, the 44-year-old Nureyev starred as the King in the 1982 North American stage revival of *The King and I*. "He couldn't dance anymore," says Pickett, "and he never could act. It was just awful. I took him to dinner opening night at Umberto's on Hornby Street and a woman came to the table and started in with, 'Oh, I just loved all those little Chinese children you had in your show!' I thought, 'Uh oh, lady. You're in trouble.' And then she said, 'Oh, they were so *cute*!' And I thought, 'Lady, now's the time to go or else you're going to be crucified.' But she didn't go.

"Nureyev abruptly stood up, sending knives and forks clattering all over the place, and threw his serviette on the table. He said: 'Lady, the next time I come to town, I'll bring nothing *but* a bunch of fucking little Chinese children and maybe *that'll* make you happy, even if everybody else *hates them*!' She immediately started whimpering, 'Ohhh,

ohhh!' and fled the place. Umberto Menghi ran over with a cooler of Dom Perignon. I started saying, 'Rudy, you can't do that. You can't *do* it.' He just looked at me and smiled and said, 'Who got the champagne?'

"I liked him through all that," Pickett declares. "I liked the strangest people. I liked the others, too, of course, but the people who were a problem were the ones I liked the best."

Pride and Prejudice

Since the days of vaudeville, African-American performers featured prominently on playbills. Sammy Davis Jr.'s apprenticeship with the Will Mastin Trio comes to mind, as does Louis Armstrong's rise to critical, commercial and cultural distinction. Regardless of the performer's stature, however, African-American entertainers endured the same humiliations wherever they ventured in North America throughout most of the 20th century, Vancouver being no exception.

"There's a famous photograph of Louis Armstrong sitting on his luggage in the lobby of the Devonshire Hotel," says big-band leader Dal Richards, Vancouver's sultan of swing since the late 1930s. "He went to the Hotel Vancouver and they weren't accepting 'coloured people.' That picture was taken across the street in the lobby of the Devonshire Hotel at Georgia and

Camping on his luggage after being refused admission to the Devon-shire Hotel in 1942, jazz superstar Louis Armstrong couldn't escape the discrimination meted out to all black entertainers in pre-1960s Vancouver. *Sev Morin Collection*

Opera diva Marian Anderson was used to standing ovations, but was surprised to get one when she showed up to watch a hockey game at the old PNE Forum.

THE ORPHEUM

B | 32 | 7

SOUND AND VISION

A BACKSTAGE VANCOUVER PRODUCTION

SEPTEMBER 21 7:30 PM

CHAPTER TWO

Patrons are required to abide by the Terms & Conditions outlined on the reverse of this ticket

B ADMIT ONE

VANCOUVER CITY CENTRE

NO ADMITTANCE AFTER CURTAIN RAISED

NO EXCEPTIONS

Hornby." It was 1942 and Armstrong was an established and internationally recognized jazz trumpeter and recording artist. He had appeared on Broadway and in half a dozen Hollywood films. He'd had hit songs on the charts for nearly a decade. None of these things made a bit of difference. "There was real racial tension and it wasn't only in the United States," says Red Robinson. "As Canadians, we sometimes smugly like to say, 'Well, we didn't have discrimination.' Bullshit. We were not clean. We were not superior to our American cousins. We were just as damned bad."

"The whole thing was just awful, just terrible," says Pickett. "Normally, I handled the accommodations and I never, ever asked the Hotel Vancouver or the Hotel Georgia to put up black performers in their hotels because I knew it wasn't going to happen. One time, Katherine Dunham, the famous dancer, came to town with a company of 30 and her manager had handled the whole thing. I didn't even know she was coming. I met them at the train in a taxi and she said, 'We're at the Hotel Vancouver.' I didn't want to say, 'Lady, you're not at the Hotel Vancouver because they don't take blacks.' So I thought, 'Okay, let's see what happens.' Everybody piled into five taxis and pulled up at the Hotel Vancouver. 'Nope, sorry,' they said. Then the Hotel Georgia. Same thing. I told her later, 'Look, I'm sorry you had to go through that. I knew it was going to happen but I thought maybe your name was big enough to change things.' Obviously, it wasn't.

"During the late 1930s, opera singer Marian Anderson was the most famous black person in the world. She came here three days before her show and was at our house having tea. My father, who was retired at that point and not really into show business, said, 'Miss Anderson, have you ever seen a hockey game?' When she said, 'No, I never have,' he said, 'Well, it's Canada's national sport and there is a hockey game tonight. Would you like to go?' She said, 'Oh, I'd love to.' I thought, 'Oh, shit, what's going to happen here?' Anyway, I stayed out of it."

A limousine picked up Anderson and Pickett's father Fred and delivered the pair to the PNE Forum. As Anderson

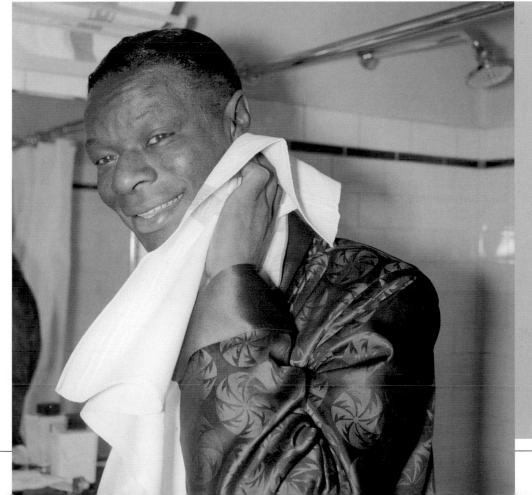

The colour bar at Vancouver hotels was finally broken by velvet-voiced Nat King Cole, who was admitted to the Hotel Georgia in 1958.
Vancouver Public Library VPL S-59973 *The Province*

entered the building, Pickett recalls, "The whole place stood up and applauded. She nearly died. She didn't think anybody would know her but they did. She was thrilled to death and so was my dad. But he didn't know what was going to happen next." What happened next was a lot of jostling as people queued up for autographs. "The whole building was on her side and everybody wanted to shake her hand; everybody wanted an autograph," says Pickett. "It took them half an hour to get out of the building after the game was finished. And though she'd never seen a hockey game, she loved it. My father said she was screaming and applauding. He couldn't believe it." Both of Anderson's concerts subsequently sold out as people who had been at the game tried to get last-minute tickets. Regardless, she still couldn't get a room at any of the city's "better" establishments.

When African-American actor, singer, activist, athlete and scholar Paul Robeson was invited to sing at the Fourth Canadian Convention of the International Union of Mine, Mill and Smelter Workers in Vancouver in February 1952, after defying the House Committee on Un-American Activities by refusing to sign an anti-communist declaration, American authorities seized Robeson's passport and denied him permission to leave the US. The convention heard Robeson sing over the telephone and promised to organize a concert at the Peace Arch border at Blaine, Washington. On May 18, 1952, Robeson stood on the back of a flatbed truck in front of 40,000 and, accompanied by pianist Lawrence Brown, sang and spoke for 45 minutes in support of defiance and solidarity. Included among the spirituals, folk songs and labour songs was the bass vocalist's trademark standard, "Old Man River." The event was commemorated with a 50th anniversary concert at the Peace Arch on May 18, 2002.

It would be 1958 before an African-American, namely Nat "King" Cole, was given a room at an upscale Vancouver hotel. "I knew him," says Pickett, "and I thought it was disgraceful that the two main hotels in Vancouver refused to accept black guests. So I said to Nat: 'Let's do a test in favour of black people. Will you do me a favour and go to the Georgia Hotel and ask for a room?' He said, 'Sure.' So I booked him into the Georgia, thinking that as soon as he walked up to the desk and they saw he was black, the desk clerk would say, 'I'm sorry.' But he went in, signed in and headed upstairs to his room. He told me later, 'There was no problem.' But that was the first time. I said to Nat, 'You've broken a spell. They wouldn't let any black people in until now.' I tell ya, it was murder. That one event changed everything."

The Blue Angel

Of the countless entertainment icons Hugh Pickett encountered during his career, his favourite was Marlene Dietrich, whom he met through convoluted circumstances. While working as an usher at the Colonial Theatre in 1930, he caught the performer's breakthrough film, *The Blue Angel*, a racy drama that most North American theatres refused to show. "In those days, the Capitol got the first-run pictures," recalls Pickett. "But they couldn't run it because you weren't allowed to show the inside of a woman's thigh and the picture consisted almost entirely of Marlene's bare legs!" Instead, the Colonial picked up the film for a pittance and Pickett was instantly smitten. "She was not the kind of woman you fell in love with. In fact, her character was a whore and awful to everybody. But I loved her."

Almost three decades later, Pickett procured a letter of introduction to Dietrich from Sir John Gielgud, in exchange for putting up the British actor's visiting friend in Vancouver. In 1959, Pickett got the letter into Dietrich's hands via a Vancouver dancer performing with her. He promptly found himself having a 1 a.m. dinner with Marlene Dietrich in Las Vegas.

In October 1964, Pickett brought Dietrich to Vancouver to appear at

Hugh Pickett welcomes Marlene Dietrich to the Vancouver Airport in 1964, 34 well-preserved years after the star and her glamorous gams first caught his eye in *The Blue Angel*. Hugh Pickett Collection

Opposite: One of Hugh Pickett's most treasured pieces of memorabilia is this signed photograph of Marlene Dietrich. Hugh Pickett Collection

Showing off his matchless collection of show bills, Pickett shudders to recall how, as a teenage stage rat at the old Colonial Theatre, he incinerated a mountain of priceless posters archived in the basement.

Hugh Pickett Collection *Vancouver Sun*

two sold-out shows at the Queen Elizabeth Theatre. "Something happened that never happened to anybody else," he recalls. "The whole audience ran down the aisles, from the balcony and everywhere. The main floor was jammed with people. She got quite a surprise when she came out from behind the curtain to take another bow and the whole place was standing there."

Perhaps even more memorable was the entourage's stop after the performance at Hy's Encore, Hornby Street's steakhouse to the stars. "On the way to Hy's for dinner, Marlene stopped in front of the hotel and signed autographs for half an hour," Pickett remembers. "Finally, I got her into the limo and then she spent another half an hour signing autographs in front of Hy's. Once we got inside, she ordered latke. When the maître d' said they didn't have it, she said, 'How can you be a restaurant with a Jewish name and not serve a traditional Jewish dish?' The maître d' explained that the cooks were Chinese. Well, Marlene, who was a wonderful cook, went into the kitchen and taught them how to make latke. It's still on the menu today."

Pickett would go on to manage Dietrich's career for the next 12 years. "I took her to Chicago, New York, everywhere," he says. "Meanwhile, I was still trying to run a business in Vancouver. And my staff at Famous Artists hated her. They'd say, 'Oh God, he's off with that German again.' Marlene used to introduce me by saying, 'This man is the biggest idiot who ever lived. He fell in love with the woman in *The Blue Angel*, for Chrissake!'"

As it turned out, Pickett was far from the biggest idiot Dietrich had ever met. During an engagement in Ottawa in 1969—Pickett organized a weeklong stint for Dietrich at the National Arts Centre with Burt Bacharach playing piano alongside a 26-piece orchestra—the pair went to dinner with then-Canadian Prime Minister Pierre Elliott Trudeau. "When we finally left to go back to the hotel, she said, 'How did Canada ever elect him? He should be the dogcatcher.'"

Bedridden for the last 12 years of her life, Dietrich died of kidney failure in Paris in 1992. "The last thing she did was in Australia in 1975," Pickett remembers. "She was 74 at the time and she shouldn't have gone. She and I'd had a fight. I told her it wasn't going to work and that she was crazy to do it; but she did it anyway. I really loved her and had a really good time with her, though we had a lot of fights. At that point, though, she really needed the money. She was flat broke. Her daughter's family just took her. It was a helluva shame."

In what could be interpreted as either a pre-emptive strike or a genuine act of forgiveness, she willed the city of Berlin—the home she had abandoned, decried and shunned during the rise of Nazism 60 years earlier—her 300,000-piece memorabilia collection, valued at roughly $11 million. Ten years later, city fathers named Marlene Dietrich an honourary citizen, hoping the declaration "would symbolize the city of Berlin's reconciliation with her."

Marlene Dietrich wasn't the only one at odds with Berlin in the 1940s. Nazi forces invaded Poland on September 1, 1939, and Britain declared war on Germany two days later. Canada, being a Commonwealth nation, entered the fray on September 10. Vancouver Harbour was placed in the hands of the Royal Canadian Navy and artillery embankments were constructed at Point Grey, Point Atkinson, Ferguson Point and Steveston, as well as beneath the First Narrows Bridge. The country had officially entered World War II. Life, however, somehow went on.

The first season of Theatre Under the Stars opened in Stanley Park's Malkin Bowl in the summer of 1940 with performances of *The Geisha*, *As You Like It* and *A Midsummer Night's Dream*. Reserved seats went for 50 cents; unreserved seats were 25 cents. In 1943, the Vancouver Art Gallery hosted the 33rd Annual Exhibition of the BC Society of Fine Arts. Among the works were six Emily Carr paintings, available for $50 each. The following year, radio station CKNW began broadcasting around the clock and became the first transmitter in the country to air news reports every hour on the hour.

Movies were not only making the most money, they were paying the most money. Aspiring actors descended on Hollywood and the Golden Age of Theatre gave way to the Golden Age of Film, as studios cranked out product at a staggering rate. Almost by default, live entertainment became the domain of musicians and all-round entertainers: showroom performers who could sing, dance, crack jokes and keep an audience amused. Some, such as Bob Hope

Dal Richards and His Orchestra often played the Orpheum when they weren't previously engaged at the Hotel Vancouver's Panorama Roof. City of Vancouver Archives CVA 1184-2313

THE ORPHEUM

B 32 7

CHAPTER THREE

SWINGIN' PARTY

A BACKSTAGE VANCOUVER PRODUCTION

SEPTEMBER 21 7:30 PM

Patrons are required to abide by the Terms & Conditions outlined on the reverse of this ticket.

B ADMIT ONE

VANCOUVER CITY CENTRE

NO ADMITTANCE AFTER CURTAIN RAISED

NO EXCEPTIONS

and Bing Crosby, worked both sides of the fence, appearing in movies while continuing to perform in person.

In the meantime, innovative and unproven disciplines were emerging that required a degree of audience attentiveness hitherto unknown outside the highbrow worlds of formal theatre and classical music. Jazz had been attracting progressively larger audiences since the heyday of flappers in the 1920s. Ever more experimental and improvisational, the form was considered crude and unconventional by "serious" musicians. What's more, it was inextricably linked to black American culture, lending it a sinister reputation propagated by bigotry and ignorance. Its devotees were, therefore, almost exclusively its black progenitors, save for a smattering of liberal-minded white intellectuals. Jazz was subsequently marginalized not because of what it was but because of what it represented. All that changed with the arrival of swing.

The Kings of Swing

"In the 1930s, we were all scrambling," says Vancouver's legendary big-band leader and saxman Dal Richards. "That's the only word for it. We were all young, just starting out in the business. Swing arrived in 1935, when I was 17 years old, and it had a powerful influence on me. One evening, I was listening to the radio and heard Benny Goodman and His Orchestra broadcasting from the Palomar Ballroom in Los Angeles. I thought, 'My God! What is that?' I couldn't believe my ears."

A meeting of bandleaders: Lawrence Welk and Dal Richards.
Dal Richards Collection

Born in 1918, Richards was raised in Vancouver's Marpole district. When he was nine, he tripped and fell on a slingshot while running down the street: an accident that resulted in the loss of his left eye. Confined to a darkened room for several months, Richards grew increasingly despondent until his mother and "a wise old country doctor" steered him toward music as a means of catharsis. "I still remember my mother taking me to the Paramount Theatre on a Saturday night to meet Arthur Delamont, leader of the Kitsilano Boys Band," says Richards. "He was my saviour." Delamont, a fearsome taskmaster and disciplinarian, was revered for training budding musicians and conducting a world-class youth orchestra that regularly cleaned up at international competitions, including the 1933 Chicago World's Fair, a coup that netted the band a trip to Britain, where they toured and recorded for the BBC and Decca Records. "He's the only reason I'm talking to you now."

A fan of dance bands, Richards formed his own outfit in the early 1930s while still in high school. "Bands prior to Goodman didn't swing, per se," he says. "They played popular dance music with a beat but not with Goodman's approach, which was actually the black approach. It's where the blues, rhythm and blues, and rock and roll all started. You can almost pinpoint it to a red-light district in New Orleans called Storyville, where cathouses provided the entertainment. That's where guys like King Oliver and Louis Armstrong got their start. It developed out of Dixieland when all these musicians headed to places like Chicago and Memphis and met black arrangers who were used to writing for big bands. I thought, 'I've got to get into this somehow.' So I bought myself a saxophone and started playing golf clubs around the community. All of a sudden, I was making $10 a weekend. I was rich! That was a lot of money in the 1930s."

In 1937, Vancouver's Palomar Supper Club opened at the corner of Georgia and Burrard, featuring Sandy DeSantis and His Orchestra.

Richards (right) stands beside mentor Arthur Delamont at an appearance of the Kitsilano Alumni Band. Delamont initiated the Kitsilano Boys Band in 1928.
Dal Richards Collection

"Sandy created quite an impression," says Richards. "Although he wasn't a writer, he copied his favourite Goodman arrangements and encouraged people to buy the records. He made quite a splash on the dancing public and was broadcast on CBC Radio, which was the big time in those days." The 21-year-old Richards joined DeSantis's band on sax and clarinet but soon found himself leading the orchestra, after DeSantis and club owner Hymie Singer had a falling out. "That was typical of Hymie," Richards says with a chuckle. "On the strength of seeing me play a little bit of clarinet, he promoted me as 'Canada's Artie Shaw at the Palomar.'"

Luck struck again when Vancouver swing sensation Mart Kenney collected his orchestra and headed east to take up residency at Toronto's Royal York Hotel in 1940, leaving a plum vacancy at the Hotel Vancouver's Panorama Roof. "I got a call to go down and audition," recalls Richards. "It was the thrill of a lifetime." Richards and his band got the gig and kept it for a quarter century—a North American record for a hotel-ballroom bandleader—relinquishing it only when Beatlemania all but swept big bands out of existence in the mid-1960s. Equally noteworthy is that Richards has played every consecutive New Year's since his first at the Cinderella Ballroom at 11th and Main in 1936. "I have more of an appreciation for that era now than I did back then," he says. "When you're working, you don't get to see as much. You don't get the broad picture. You have to step back."

Stepping back has given Richards a healthy perspective on the great talents, and even greater eccentrics, he has encountered over the years. "A lot of the stars stayed at the Hotel Vancouver or across the street at the Hotel Georgia when they visited Vancouver," he says, "and they'd come to the Panorama Roof for dinner. I got to know a lot of them that way. It was interesting because it was different than meeting them professionally. At dinner, they would be in a social mood and they all had different personalities.

"I only met Benny Goodman once," he says of the man who changed his life, "and it was under unusual circumstances." Indeed, when fellow saxophonist and American bandleader Les Brown came to town with his orchestra to play the grand opening of the Four Seasons Hotel in 1975, Richards, attending as a guest, was accosted during the intermission by Pickett. "Hugh grabbed me and said, 'Do you know Les Brown?'" Richards remembers. "I said, 'Yeah, sort of.' And Hugh said, 'Well, I've got Benny Goodman in tow. Will you introduce him to Les Brown?' It turned out that Goodman was in town playing the Queen Elizabeth Theatre that night with a small band that included [pioneering jazz pianist and vocalist] Stan Kenton and he wanted to meet Brown. I said to Hugh, 'Well, what's the matter with you? Why can't you introduce them? You brought him here.' And Hugh said, 'We're

Mart Kenney, once proclaimed "the premier Canadian dance band leader of the 20th century," started his career in Vancouver.
City of Vancouver Archives
CVA 99-2742

Opposite: In an era where popular musicians were generally well behaved, temperamental drummer Buddy Rich was a notable exception. Here he rests between sets at a 1969 gig in Vancouver.
Ken Oakes *Vancouver Sun*

not speaking.' And that was that. But Goodman was like that. If something about you bothered him, that was the end of it; you were out. So I introduced Benny Goodman to Les Brown. And those, it seems, were the first and last words ever spoken between the two. Goodman treated Brown like a junior and the animosity was evident."

Equally temperamental was famed and furious drummer Buddy Rich. He never missed a chance. "When Buddy was having his third heart attack, paramedics strapped an oxygen mask to his face and asked if he was allergic to anything," Richards recalls. "Right there on the stretcher, Buddy pulled off the oxygen mask and said, 'Yeah, country-and-western music.'" Yet mention the drummer's name to long-time Vancouver music aficionados and you instantly spark wide-eyed accounts of a 1956 "drum-off" between Rich and equally renowned traps-man Gene Krupa at the Georgia Auditorium. On a *Jazz at the Philharmonic* touring bill organized by noted LA jazz producer and promoter Norman Granz, and emceed by 19-year-old deejay Red Robinson, the percussive pair brought down the house.

"The lineup that night was Ella Fitzgerald, Lester Young, Oscar Peterson, Barney Kessel, Charlie Shavers, Flip Phillips and Roy Eldridge," says Robinson, "as well as Buddy Rich and the Gene Krupa Trio. I had the pleasure of standing on the stage and saying, 'Ladies and gentlemen, the Battle of the Drums featuring Gene Krupa'—and the spotlight goes on Gene—'and Buddy Rich'—and the spotlight goes on Buddy. And then they started. It was unbelievable. I'd never seen anything like it. Nobody had."

Born in 1917 to a family of New York entertainers, Buddy Rich made his vaudeville debut at 18 months and was known as "Baby Traps" by his seventh birthday. Having worked with Bunny Berigan, Artie Shaw and Tommy Dorsey, Rich developed a reputation as one of the finest drummers in the business and, with financial help from fellow Dorsey alumnus Frank Sinatra, formed his own band in 1946. "We all know Buddy was a temperamental, volatile and outspoken guy," says Richards, "and that was reflected both in his personality and throughout his entire playing career."

BACKSTAGE VANCOUVER

Along with Buddy Rich, Gene Krupa was one of the only drummers in history capable of single-handedly attracting a big crowd. Autographing records and drum heads in Vancouver, 1941. David H. Buchan

Richards remembers a particular evening at Isy's Supper Club on West Georgia, where Rich was in the midst of a week-long Vancouver engagement: "There was an infamous local hooker by the name of Minka, who had a second-floor suite above the Orpheum at the northeast corner of Smythe and Granville. She went to all the shows and all the clubs constantly, hooking musicians. She was a good-looking woman, well-spoken, well-dressed and appeared to be a rather astute business person, as well. But when she went to the clubs, she was more interested in promoting herself than looking at the shows."

Having already ingratiated herself to Rich in her professional capacity earlier in the week, Minka made the mistake of taking him for granted during a performance a few nights later. "She always had a table to the front and centre of the stage, wherever she went," says Richards, "and this one night she was at Isy's, not paying the

slightest bit of attention to the band. She was just talking away among her clientele to the degree that she was disturbing Buddy while he was playing. Now, unlike Krupa, Buddy had his drum kit in front of the band, so all this inattention was going on right in front of him. The next thing you know, he stopped the band midway through a number—which is something you never ever do—and walked from behind his kit to the lip of the stage. You could have heard a pin drop. He said to her, 'You shut the fuck up!' Then he went back behind his drum kit and continued playing."

Minka was suitably chastised but was soon back at her tricks. Not long afterwards, Richards recalls, Sammy Davis Jr. was in town performing several nights at the Cave. "The first time I saw Sammy, he was at the Palomar with the Will Mastin Trio, which included his father and uncle," says Richards, referring to the troupe Davis got his start with in 1928 at the age of three. (Mastin was Sammy's "uncle" onstage only, not a relative; in the late 1930s, Orpheum manager Ivan Ackery scored the Trio's services for a midnight show, paying them $15 each). "I used to have breakfast or lunch with the three of them and got to know Sammy a little bit. By the time he was headlining the Cave in the late fifties, he was a major star in his own right and the story is that Minka had the hots for Sammy and had been following him around all week but he wasn't paying any attention to her. In fact,

Above: Sammy Davis Jr. looks over the shoulders of deejay Monty McFarlane and his wife Arline at the Cave Supper Club, the hottest and tackiest club on the Hornby Street strip. Monty McFarlane Collection

Living up to the "Girls! Girls! Girls!" line posted on its marquee, Isy's Supper Club presents the dance-hall group Stare in 1969. Deni Eagland *Vancouver Sun*

SOUVENIR
PROGRAMME

Bing Crosby Show
SPONSORED BY PHILCO
CO-OPERATING WITH
SUNSET MEMORIAL CENTRE
FORUM, 8 p.m., WEDNESDAY, SEPTEMBER 22nd, 1948

25c

he wouldn't have anything to do with her. So, on his last night at the Cave, she bought tickets for a table right in front of the stage, sat there by herself, and when Sammy came out, she brought a newspaper, held it up in front of her and read it throughout Sammy's entire act."

The Crooners

As headlining performers frequently travelled with little more than a rhythm section and a musical director/piano player, they hired local musicians to accompany them when they arrived in town. Richards and his orchestra were, therefore, enlisted to back up any number of stars, including Bing Crosby, Bob Hope, Rosemary Clooney, Rudy Vallee, Lena Horne, Liberace and Frank Sinatra Jr.

Crosby, in particular, is well-remembered for lending a hand in opening East Vancouver's Sunset Memorial Centre (now the Sunset Community Centre) at 404 East 51st Avenue. Although fundraising efforts to build the facility commenced in 1945, it wasn't until Crosby took the stage at the PNE Forum on September 22, 1948, that enough money was raised to complete the structure. Almost half the cost of the centre, an estimated $60,000, was drummed up on that single evening, when the entertainer consented to broadcast his Philco-sponsored network radio program *The Bing Crosby Show* from the Forum (with special guest Ray Milland) and donate all proceeds to the fund.

"Bing was here for several days and rehearsed the show for two days beforehand at the Orpheum, beginning at nine o'clock in the morning," says Richards. "In fact, the CBC taped the rehearsals and pieced together the best parts for broadcast rather than use the stuff from the Forum, which had very poor acoustics. Bing and his entourage were here three or four days, altogether. You'd see him and he'd say hello but you never got very close to him. There was no camaraderie at all between him and the local musicians. He had his own gang."

Regardless, Crosby (born in Tacoma, Washington, in 1903) was not altogether aloof and one of his "gang," guitarist Perry Botkin, was pals with Dal. "Perry was close to Bing," says Richards, "and Perry and I just seemed to get along. He told me some crazy stories about Crosby, mostly involving women." It was through Botkin that Richards was able to cajole Crosby into showing up at Oscar's Steakhouse, a late-night hangout during the post-war years that not only catered to visiting celebrities but had walls adorned with photographs of stars, invariably posed with the proprietor's arm wrapped around their shoulders. "After the shows, everybody ended up at Oscar's

Before Elvis or the Beatles set foot in Vancouver, adoring mobs forced Bing Crosby to employ serious muscle.
Vancouver Public Library
VPL 80676-A

Opposite: At the pinnacle of his crooning career, Bing Crosby found time to play a charity for Vancouver's first community centre.
Red Robinson Collection

because there weren't very many late-night places in those days," says Richards, noting that the exceptions included bring-your-own-bottle joints such as Vi's Steakhouse on Union Street, Love's Cafe on Granville, Monty's Spare Ribs on Seymour and Jeannie Flynn's—the latter located across the street from Monty's and popularly known as "Nigger Jean's," a title that was symptomatic of the times. "Vancouver was a small town then," says Richards, shaking his head at the recollection. "Nobody thought twice about it." (Undaunted, proprietress Jeannie Fuller Flynn went on to a career playing Aunt Jemima at the PNE.)

Meanwhile, over at Oscar's, its namesake was becoming increasingly frantic as time passed and Crosby failed to put in an appearance. "After Bing had been in town a couple of days," says Richards, "I got a call from Oscar saying, 'Dal, Bing hasn't been in. Is there anything you can do?' Oscar was devastated. He had pictures of everybody who

With his ubiquitous pipe firmly in place, the versatile Crosby enjoys a round of golf in Vancouver.
Ralph Bower

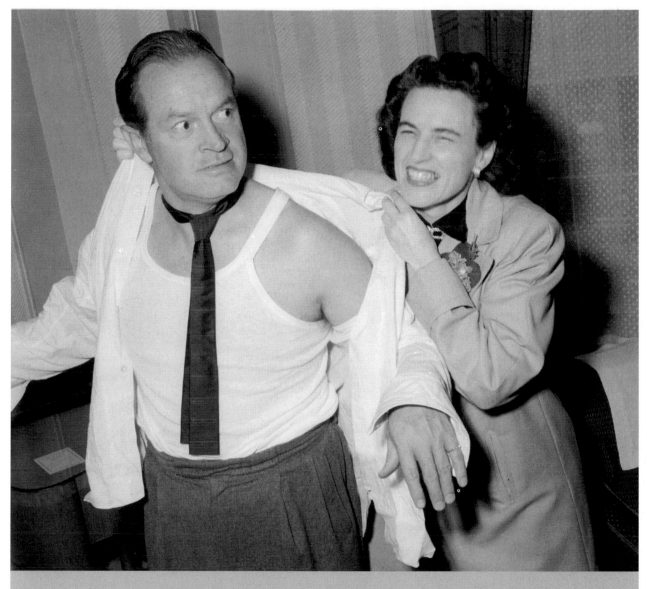

Infamous for his frugality, Bob Hope looks more than a bit reluctant giving up his shirt for charity.
Vancouver Public Library VPL S –61220 *The Province*

ever came to Vancouver on his walls, except Crosby. And Crosby was the biggest star on the planet at the time. So I told Perry about Oscar's place and he said, 'Oh, yeah, I've heard of it. Lemme see what I can do.' He came back and said, 'Yeah, let's go there after the show. Bing's got about a dozen guys and they all want to go to Oscar's around midnight.'

"By this point, I was due onstage and didn't have a chance to phone Oscar back and tell him we were coming. So after the show, I called up and said, 'Keep the place open, we're coming over,' and the woman on the other end of the line said, 'Oscar's not here. We've got him in the back. He's drunk.' Oscar was in such despair that Crosby hadn't shown up that he'd gotten completely blotto. So we went down to the restaurant and I went into the backroom, put my arm around Oscar, propped him up on my shoulder and said, 'Don't say anything.' We went out, I said, 'Mr. Crosby, this is Oscar, your host' and they snapped the picture. I took him back to the backroom and he passed out cold. He couldn't believe it when he saw the picture. He didn't remember a thing."

Crosby's contemporary and frequent sidekick, Bob Hope, came into Richards's life later, when the comedian began appearing in town at corporate functions in the early 1970s. "The first time was at the Hotel Vancouver," says Richards. "Bob would come here for one-night-only special events. The first time I met him, we were rehearsing in the ballroom and suddenly I was losing the band's attention. I looked around and Bob Hope was crossing the ballroom floor. I remember thinking, 'What a multifaceted entertainer. The history of the 20th century is the history of Bob Hope.' But all those stories about him being cheap are true."

Richards's orchestra played for Hope on several occasions and evidence of the entertainer's notorious frugality were apparent from the beginning. "Many of the stars would bring along their musical directors with charts for 15-piece bands," Richards explains, "meaning that, on those occasions, I was playing in the band as opposed to leading it. So we're at the first rehearsal and Bob's musical director says, 'With the score for letter A, Bob's voice has lowered a bit so transpose that down a tone.' Okay, so we do that. 'Now, letter E,' he says, 'cut that out because Bob doesn't do that dance anymore. Cut from letter E to L.' And the rehearsal continued on like that. By then, we realized that the musical director has already done this with a hundred other orchestras before us because the charts looked like chicken scratch. And so it went throughout all the numbers for the show. Meanwhile, the sponsor is paying for the rehearsal and it's going on twice as long as it's supposed to. Bob could have had all the charts with the changes copied for a few hundred dollars but instead, no, no, no. And they were going around the country like this!"

Hope was equally stingy at home. When Richards and his wife Muriel visited Frank Sinatra's former house in Palm Springs after it had been purchased by business tycoon and fellow Kitsilano Boys Band member Jimmy Pattison following Sinatra's death, he encountered yet another example of Hope's parsimonious nature: "We were going in a cab from Frank's place to the airport and the cab driver pointed out Bob Hope's house and muttered to himself, 'Cheap bastard.' I said, 'Why do you say that?' And the cabbie said, 'Whenever he brings in scriptwriters from Hollywood to work for a couple of days, he'll pay the cab fare but not the tip.'"

As for Sinatra himself, says Richards, "He was the man." First appearing in Vancouver at the Beacon Theatre in 1936 with the Hoboken Four, Sinatra returned to the city for several performances over the years, including a 1957 show at the Forum. "Frank almost always brought his own musicians," says Richards, "but not the first time. On that occasion, he brought his key men—Nelson Riddle was the bandleader—and selected the best musicians in the city. Frank liked our musicians and everyone wanted to play with him." As for spending three days at Sinatra's old digs, Richards says, "It was like living my youth all over again. The walls were lined with sheet-music covers, awards and hundreds of pictures of celebrities. His golf clubs were still sitting in the corner and the bar was still stocked with Jack Daniel's. You could feel Sinatra when you walked in there. It was fabulous."

Richards' brushes with fame, however, were not always quite so fabulous. Old-time vaudevillian Eddie Cantor was a fine humanitarian who coined the term "March of Dimes" in 1938 and campaigned for the fight against polio. But he was a second-rate talent, at best. By the mid-1930s, his film career had tanked and he returned to live performances, mostly to be recognized. "He was here for a few days in the early forties," Richards recalls. "There was an elevated area at the entrance to the Panorama Roof when you got off the elevator and Eddie Cantor would always pause there and look at me. He wouldn't enter until I'd say from the bandstand, 'Hi, Eddie! C'mon in, Eddie Cantor! C'mon in, Eddie!' He wanted everybody to know he was there. Eddie Cantor was famous for a few minutes. Rudy Vallee did the same thing."

His star long since in decline, Eddie Cantor still craved VIP treatment whenever he appeared at the Hotel Vancouver's Panorama Roof. Vancouver Public Library VPL 59767 *The Province*

Vallee, a bandleader and actor best remembered for singing through a megaphone on the heels of his catchphrase

Bob Hope returns to Vancouver in 1986. "The history of the 20th century is the history of Bob Hope." —Dal Richards. Craig Hodge

"Heigh Ho, Everybody!", was by all accounts insufferably arrogant. In the 1970s, for example, he demanded that the Los Angeles Chamber of Commerce rename a street near his home "Rue de Vallée." Shortly before his death in 1986, he boasted, "In 84 years of life, I've been with over 145 women and girls."

"What a character," Richards says, pityingly. "We played for him and he did all the old songs but his voice was gone, so mostly he just told stories about various stars he'd known. One time during a show he said, 'I'd like to conduct an arrangement of "Ebb Tide" by Morton Gould.' No one in the band expected it or knew what he was talking about. It hadn't been mentioned, let alone rehearsed. Then he turned around, pressed the play button on a tape recorder and started conducting a tape deck. The band just about died. We all just sat there looking at the floor. It was sad."

Liberace, on the other hand, was simply ebullient. "He was one of the nicest guys I've ever spent time with," says Richards. "In 1975, we played the Queen Elizabeth Theatre for a week with a big band, plus the Vancouver Symphony Orchestra string session. At the end of the run, he threw a backstage party for everybody, including the stagehands, and gave me a pair of cufflinks. We did eight shows and his routine never varied, not once. At the same time during each performance, he'd say that he was sending out a special request and read off a pair of seat numbers with the name of the couple sitting there. Then he'd say, 'They're celebrating their 50th wedding anniversary this evening and this one is for them.' Then he'd play 'It's Impossible.'"

Perhaps the oddest duo to share the limelight with Richards at the Panorama Roof was singing cowboy Roy Rogers and his horse Trigger. "It was 1946 and the Beacon Theatre still had vaudeville," says Richards. "One week, Roy and Trigger were the featured act and the Beacon's manager, who was a very promotions-oriented guy, thought it would be a great idea to bring Trigger into a nightclub. So they brought him up in the freight elevator and Roy walked him through the club."

Another entertainer who long outstayed his glory days, Rudy Vallee once astounded the Richards band by conducting a tape deck onstage. Courtesy of Eleanor Vallee

It took a nervy promotions manager and a skookum freight elevator to get singing cowpoke Roy Rogers and his inseparable mount Trigger up to the Hotel Vancouver's Panorama Roof in 1946. Dal Richards Collection

Always the consummate pro, Liberace's Vancouver appearances were as elaborately designed as his wardrobe (and microphone). Ralph Bower

Juliette Augustina Sysak, aka "Our Pet Juliette," (left) started her run as Canada's favourite songbird by appearing with Dal Richards at the tender age of 13. Here she helps Dal celebrate 10 years "on top of the town." *Vancouver Sun*

Opposite: Juliette in 1959. At 32 years old she had logged almost 20 years in the public eye. Henry Fox

The Divas

With his light baritone, Richards generally handled the orchestra's vocal chores himself. In 1940, however, the Orpheum's Ivan Ackery convinced him to hire a "girl singer" in the tradition of Anita O'Day, Jo Stafford and Peggy Lee. "Ivan hired local bands to appear at the Orpheum on Friday nights for 40-minute shows between the movies," says Richards. "Sandy DeSantis played some Fridays, as did Earl Hill. I got a call from Ivan to come down and play, which was a thrill, and he came to me and said, 'Dal, I can't help noticing you don't have a girl singer. Well, I heard a girl at the Kitsilano Showboat the other night and she's just 13 years old. You really should hear her.' I just kinda looked at him. I mean, the Kitsilano Showboat was amateur hour. But I went and listened to her and she could sing, all right. So we put her in a show in June 1940 and she sang 'There Will Always Be an England,' which was a huge hit during World War II. She brought the house down. It was Juliette and that was her first professional appearance."

The daughter of Polish-Ukrainian immigrants would spend the next two years with Dal Richards and His Orchestra before hosting her own CBC Radio program at age 15. Relocating to Toronto in 1954, she then launched *The Juliette Show* on CBC-TV in 1956, a Saturday-night staple that aired coast-to-coast for more than a decade. In the meantime, there was the issue of a schoolgirl performing in a nightclub. (Juliette rode her bicycle to the Hotel Vancouver, where doormen dutifully saluted her and parked it.) Although few establishments were licensed to sell alcohol, and it was illegal to sell hard liquor by the drink in BC until 1953, nightclubs were generally recognized as "bottle clubs," meaning patrons could brown-bag their own booze and buy mix and ice from vendors. "The Canadian Pacific Railway, which was running the Hotel Vancouver, had difficulty with me hiring an underage

person," recounts Richards. "Even though there wasn't any liquor in the Roof in theory, of course, there actually was. It was a bottle-under-the-table situation and they had concerns about the police raiding the club, which they did once in a while. I say they 'raided' the clubs, which means they put on their hats, walked through and said, 'How are you tonight, Dal?' Nevertheless, it was a concern."

The matter was resolved after Richards had a chat with Juliette's parents and agreed to become her legal guardian in the event of a lawsuit. "Of course, that didn't lead to anything," says Richards. "We had a system in the Roof that enabled us to prepare for a visitation by the police force. Because they had to walk by the bell captain and come up 15 floors by elevator, the bell captain would immediately phone the head waiter in the Roof. At that point, we would get the signal on the bandstand and stop whatever we were playing and start in with, 'Roll Out the Barrel.' That was the cue for everybody to check their bottles away. It didn't happen very frequently, maybe a couple of times a year."

Following Juliette's departure, Lorraine McAllister joined the band and, in 1951, became Richards's first wife. "Lorraine was an inspiration to me," he says. "I admired her professionalism and success, and she was an excellent musician, pianist and singer." Moreover, she was an actress who appeared on television and at Theatre Under the Stars. The pair had a daughter, Dallas (later a successful Victoria realtor), and continued to perform together throughout the 1950s and 1960s. The front cover of Richards's first album, 1964's *Dance Date With Dal*, features a spectacular photograph of the couple dressed to the nines at the entrance to the Panorama Roof—the height of martini chic. "It was supposed to be a 'live' album recorded at the Roof," he says. "But, in fact, it was recorded in an empty Roof and they dubbed in the crowd noises later."

Another great female singer provided a role model, however fleetingly, for the pair's young daughter in the early 1960s. "Lena Horne was playing the Cave and we struck it off," says Richards of the jazz chanteuse, who was born in Brooklyn in 1917 and schooled at Harlem's famed Cotton Club under the tutelage of Cab Calloway and Duke Ellington. "Her musical director had been up to the Roof for dinner and I said, 'What are you doin' later? Why don't you come up to my place in Kerrisdale?' So they did. We had a big place at 54th and Maple in those days and Lena—what a doll!—sat in the kitchen on a stool all night and the party just swirled around her. She talked to everybody, sipping her scotch. My daughter was about 12 at the time and I didn't know it but she'd been sitting at the top of the stairs throughout the party. The next day she was snapping her gum. I said to her, 'What the heck do you think you're doing?' and she said, 'Lena Horne snaps her gum!'"

Broadway heartthrob Robert Goulet has "nothing but fond memories" of his youthful summer in Vancouver playing opposite local beauty Lorraine McCallister in *South Pacific*. Dal Richards Collection

The bandleader wasn't so lucky with Rosemary Clooney, probably best remembered for starring opposite Bing Crosby and Danny Kaye in 1954's *White Christmas*. (She was also the aunt of actor George Clooney, one of 10 pallbearers at her funeral when she died in 2002, at 74.) "We caught her at a bad time," says Richards. "We played with her for four days at the PNE. She'd just divorced from José Ferrer and she talked about her kids and the terrible life she'd had with Ferrer." Married twice to Oscar-winning actor Ferrer (1953 to 1961 and 1966 to 1967), the pair had five children before splitting for good. "Ferrer had been pretty brutal to her and she was involved in the drug scene. During one of the performances I was conducting for her at the PNE, she stopped the show. That's a no-no but she was a mean bitch at the time."

Left: Despite her demure appearance, Lena Horne (right) was the scotch-quaffing, gum-snapping life of the party. Dal Richards Collection
Rosemary Clooney (above) shares a smile with Red Robinson. Richards remembers the co-star of *White Christmas* as "a mean bitch."
Red Robinson Collection

Regardless, Clooney once recorded one of Richards's songs. "I was friends with the composer and orchestra leader Bert Lown and he used to tell me, 'Dal, write a song. I know everybody in Hollywood. I'll get somebody to play it.' I finally wrote a song called 'Love Goes on Forever' and got a call from Bert one night, saying, 'Dal, good news. Rosie likes your song! Rosemary Clooney likes your song and she's gonna record it.' Well, just about this time, Bert Lown died in his sleep. As it turned out, Rosemary had recorded 18 tunes and 16 were put on the album. Mine was on the cutting-room floor. But I was that close."

One of the most indelible impressions left on Richards was by Vancouver-born actress and singer Margaret "Peggy" Middleton, better known as Yvonne De Carlo and better still as Lily Munster of the hit TV series *The Munsters*, which aired from 1964 to 1966. Long before adopting the ghoulish kitsch, however, De Carlo (born in 1922) worked desperately to get into showbiz. "When we were playing the Palomar in the early days," says Richards, "there was a line of dancers and she was one of those dancers. She had a burning desire to be in the business. She'd say, 'Oh, I've got all the costumes. I've got the music.' She was pestering me and pestering me all the time to do the solo bit in the line. She wanted to don the top hat, white tie and tails, and dance like Fred Astaire with a cane and everything else. We never did it."

At 15, De Carlo's mother dragged the girl to Hollywood, where she won the Miss Venice Beach 1938 swimsuit contest. Failing to find stardom, however, Yvonne and her mother returned to Vancouver in 1940. Appreciating that less is more, De Carlo returned to Tinseltown and shed as many clothes as permissible at the time, appearing in a series of mostly forgettable roles playing bathing beauties before getting typecast in various states of undress. In 1944, she was voted Most Beautiful Woman in the World. In 1956, she gained credibility at last by appearing opposite Charlton Heston as Moses's wife Sephora in *The Ten Commandments*.

"In the early sixties," says Richards, "she stayed in Vancouver with Howard Hughes. They were boyfriend-girlfriend at the time and they were at a table in the Panorama Roof, just the two of them. She came over to say hello and invited me to have a drink with them during intermission. I went and Howard Hughes was sitting in tennis shoes, scruffy old jacket, no tie. Normally, they wouldn't have let him in but they didn't want to say 'No' to Howard Hughes. So I went over and she introduced me. I was there maybe 12 or 13 minutes. Hughes didn't say, 'Hello,' 'Drop dead,' 'How do you do?' He didn't say one word. Yvonne and I talked and he just sat there." Hughes returned to Vancouver in the mid-1970s with his posse of Mormons and appropriated the top two floors of the Bayshore Inn. "The lights on those floors remained on 24 hours a day," says Richards. "He considered Vancouver a safe haven."

Alexis Smith, a contemporary of De Carlo's, also got her start as a dancer. Born in Penticton in 1921, Smith's first professional job was in the 1934 ballet *Carmen* at the Hollywood Bowl. A one-time "Miss Penticton," the vivacious redhead co-starred with Cary Grant in the 1946 Cole Porter biopic *Night and Day*, though her favourite role was in director Frank Capra's 1951 musical/comedy *Here Comes the Groom* opposite Bing Crosby and Jane Wyman. Married to actor Craig Stevens in 1944 (TV private eye *Peter Gunn* from 1958 to 1961), the union lasted 49 years, until Smith's death from brain cancer in 1993. Her last role was a major one in Martin Scorsese's *The Age of Innocence*, released posthumously the same year she died.

In 1965, after a quarter century, Dal Richards and His Orchestra were let go from the Panorama Roof, replaced by a combo. "It all came to a grinding halt, I'll tell ya," he says. "In 1965, Hilton Hotels took over and there were no more big bands. I was without work. I couldn't believe it. But Elvis and the Beatles were on the charts; it was a new age and there were new tastes and preferences in music."

Vancouver-born Peggy Middleton, aka Yvonne De Carlo, was voted the "Most Beautiful Woman in the World" in 1944 but is best remembered as den mother to a mob of ghouls in the hit 1960s sitcom, *The Munsters*. MPTV.net

BACKSTAGE VANCOUVER

The 1950s were the 20th century's mid-life crisis. World War II had ended in 1945 and hatred and fear were replaced by doubt and anxiety. A new mass-market economy utilized communications technology to nurture the teen market. Life began imitating art, rather than the other way around, and entertainers were transformed from mere celebrities into role models, trendsetters and social barometers.

Between 1950 and 1960, Vancouver's population, bolstered by the baby boom and an ever-swelling suburbia, exploded from 580,000 to 825,000. The Ridge Theatre was unveiled in 1950, just as Vancouver's first atomic bomb shelter was being built in an unidentified backyard in Shaughnessy. Princess Elizabeth and Prince Philip visited the city in October 1951, and five months later, the former ascended to the throne of England.

Vancouver's first television station, CBUT, went on the air December 17, 1953, and the city's first cocktail lounge opened in the Sylvia Hotel in the summer of 1954. Streetcars were retired, the Stanley Park aquarium opened and hillside view lots in West Vancouver's exclusive British Properties were going for $2,000 to $5,000. Rock and roll hit Vancouver in the summer of 1956 with the arrival of Bill Haley and His Comets, the Hula-Hoop fad struck in 1958 and the 2,929-seat Queen Elizabeth Theatre, the city's new cultural flagship, flung open its doors in 1959.

The Ridge Theatre, at Arbutus and 16th, in its heyday.
Courtesy the Ridge Theatre

The Call of the Wild

The Hollywood film industry made a lot of people fabulously rich and famous and they didn't mind paying for exclusive getaways. Coquitlam's rustic Steelhead Lodge, a main building and cluster of log cabins along the Coquitlam River in an area once known as the Oxbow Ranch lands (now the River Springs community), proved an ideal setting. Purchased by Canadian-born Hollywood stuntman Karl Jacobs and two cousins, the site was at the end of Shaughnessy Street, shadowed by dense vine and maple clusters and overhanging cliffs, and initially unapproachable by vehicle. Jacobs built a road into the property, carrying paving stones from the river by hand and clearing the land himself before beginning construction on the living quarters. His Herculean efforts convinced his cousins to hand him full ownership of the 126 acres.

In 1939, Jacobs married Mexican-born Clara "Babe" Guiol, a second-string Hollywood starlet. Their middling film careers having petered out—Clara's biggest claim to fame was having once appeared alongside comedian Stan Laurel—the Jacobs moved to the ranch and began work on the lodge shortly after they wed. Although their careers were unremarkable, the friends and connections they made in Hollywood were not. The isolation of the retreat appealed to stars of sturdy stock and regular visitors throughout the 1940s and 1950s included Clark Gable, Carole Lombard, Roy Rogers, John Wayne, Kim Novak and Errol Flynn. Road signs to this day indicate Flynn Crescent, Gable Street and Novak Drive.

As Clara Jacobs wrote in a memoir, "I remember Clark Gable coming up. He and my brother liked to fish and catch rattlesnakes. Gable played the piano and I played the guitar and we had lots of fun. Gable was so nice and he always came by himself, no girlfriends. He just came to fish for steelhead and pike in the Coquitlam River. He would always stay for a while. Roy Rogers showed me how to twirl a rope, lassoes. Once, we all went on a boat from Vancouver with John Wayne and some girls. Steelhead Lodge was a retreat for a lot of those stars. They

A cabin at Coquitlam's Steelhead Lodge, the favourite retreat of many a Hollywood star. Courtesy Coquitlam Heritage Photos

Clara Jacobs and her husband owned and operated the Steelhead Lodge. Always dressed to the nines, Clara liked to point out that she purchased her clothes in Vancouver, not California. Courtesy Coquitlam Heritage Photos

wanted some private time and would come up. The stars would bring their own cars and brought in their own supplies. We did our cooking on an iron stove and often had wonderful steaks we got from a butcher in Coquitlam. The guests slept in the cabins but everybody ate in the lodge at a big table. I remember they would bring big dogs, which were always as high as the table.

"We always made kickapoo juice for our parties, made our own booze. We would all get stoned on it. A man named Fergie helped us look after the place. I remember he never took a bath and he would wash his underwear and hang it up in the bush. My husband was very handy and he put in the pool and built the cabin we had. We had places to play tennis and downstairs in the fishing lodge there was a ping-pong table. You had to go down all these steps into the basement. We used to dance all night. The stars who stayed with us always had dogs and cats, lots of

His popularization of Chicago blues stylings made Vancouver regular Frankie Laine one of the most well-liked performers on the planet during the 1950s. Harry Filion *Vancouver Sun*

them, and the bears, owls, raccoons and deer around the ranch used to scare them. We had plenty of snow up there and the water in the springtime was from the melted snow. We never had any doctors out there but people were stronger and more self-reliant in those days."

Clara became a familiar sight in town, driving around Coquitlam, she recalled, in a "shiny Ford roadster with a rumble seat." Always "dressed to the nines," she liked to point out that she purchased her clothes in Vancouver, not California. "I always wore sunglasses," she said, "black ones, when I drove the car. I had a lot of fur coats as well as jewellery but some of it was stolen while we were away once." Early on, Karl Jacobs installed a pulley-and-cable device for emergency exits and, indeed, the Steelhead Lodge burned down twice and was devastated more than once by flooding. The Jacobs had no children, and when Karl died in 1964, Clara sold the ranch to a gravel company.

The Birth of Cool

Although singers had always taken centre stage, they were relegated to playing second banana behind big-band leaders. All that changed when Frank Sinatra quit the Tommy Dorsey Orchestra in 1943 and struck out as a solo performer. An entire generation of vocalists followed suit, not the least of which was jazz and blues belter Frankie Laine. The Chicago-born son of Sicilian immigrants (his father was Al Capone's barber), Laine first hit Vancouver's Palomar Supper Club in 1948. He would continue to assail the city for years.

"Laine was unbelievably popular and did mostly old jazz standards and a lot of black blues," recalls author and poet Peter Trower, who was in the audience that night at the Palomar. "But the difference between him and most white singers was that he moved around on stage; he wasn't static. A lot of the old-time band singers, like Sinatra, used to stand there absolutely stiff. Laine snapped his fingers and bounced all over the place." Laine's

Legendary jazz composer Duke Ellington tightens up his trumpet section during a visit in 1953.
Vancouver Public Library VPL 60436A *The Province*

Count Basie kicks back in his Vancouver hotel room, 1952.
Vancouver Public Library VPL S-59452 *The Province*

natural inclination to groove derived directly from the black rhythm 'n' blues artists he'd witnessed in Chicago. Commercially buoyed by his rendition of Hoagy Carmichael's "Rockin' Chair," Laine would go on to accrue more than 20 gold records, give a command performance for Queen Elizabeth II and top the British charts for 18 weeks in 1953 with "I Believe" (a stretch unrivalled by even the Beatles).

"Laine was a big star who came to Vancouver all the time," says Red Robinson, who at 16 got the nod to emcee and host a Laine show at the Georgia Auditorium at the corner of Georgia and Denman. "There I am, a kid on stage with Frankie Laine and I'm thrilled out of my mind. He was a magnificent performer. Perry Como and all those guys just stood there but they called Laine 'Mr. Rhythm' because he got into it." An avid golfer, Laine could often be seen strolling the links at the Capilano Golf and Country Club during his frequent visits to Vancouver. "Frankie knows this city very well," claims Robinson. "People don't realize that, from about 1950 to 1957, he was one of the biggest performers on the planet."

"There was a 'Sing Like Frankie Laine Contest' at the Palomar one time," remembers Trower, "and Sammy Davis Jr., who was up here with the Will Mastin Trio before anybody had ever heard of him, got on stage. Davis was a great mimic and after he sang, Laine said, 'He does me better than I do!'"

Trower recalls that Billie Holiday—the intense, influential and ultimately tragic jazz stylist—was booked to perform in Vancouver in the early 1950s, "but was stopped at the border when they found a dirty opium pipe in her gear. She couldn't enter Canada. It was a very sad event." Then there was the time drum thumper Gene Krupa was arrested mid-performance. "He'd just been busted for pot in the States," says Trower, "and the border patrol came right out onto the stage and led him off. Eventually, they had to let him come back and finish the show because the crowd was going nuts.

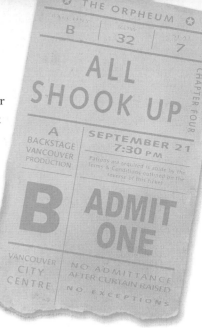

"There used to be a place called the New Orleans Club, just off Granville," Trower continues. "I've never heard anybody even mention the place in years. It was a black club, though really the only blacks around were the porters from the trains. There were a few black places in the East End but there were no mixed audiences until later. I had a friend called Mickey Walker who was a drummer and he got to know the musicians and played in the bands—a little skinny white kid playing behind these black guys—so we were allowed into the New Orleans Club. It was the first time I ever heard real blues, Basin Street blues. We were pretty much the only white people in there but there was no animosity. In fact, everybody was very kind to us."

The city's premier bop club, meanwhile, was the Jazz Cellar near Broadway and Main, which featured the most innovative artists of the day, including Ornette Coleman and Charlie Mingus, who were both "bootlegged" at the club: their performances captured on rare and illicit recordings. "A lot of them were junkies," says Trower, noting that colourful sax-and-clarinet player Art Pepper and ultra-suave trumpet blower Chet Baker were among them. "Some Vancouver musicians got hooked on dope through these famous musicians. The thinking was that you could play better when you were stoned. Chet Baker was such a junkie he ran out of veins and was shooting up in his scrotum."

"Baker was stopped by Canadian Customs on his way into the country," recollects retired *Vancouver Sun* columnist Denny Boyd. "They knew his reputation and they were going to seize his trumpet. They knew, if they didn't, he would probably pawn it to buy heroin. Then they decided maybe that was a bit brutal, so they seized the trumpet's mouthpiece, instead. This was at a time when a drug supplier in San Francisco had backhanded him in the mouth with a beer bottle a few nights earlier and knocked out all his front teeth. Nonetheless, he was a really interesting guy and had no anger against anybody. He was just as gentle as one of his trumpet solos." According to biographer James Gavin, that was true—as long as Baker had his "medicine" and an audience willing to be charmed by his stories and songs. The story of how Baker lost his teeth would be revisited and revised countless times over the years. Addicted to heroin throughout his adult life, he was known to be devious, treacherous and even violent when suffering withdrawals, due to lack of money or supplies. He died May 13, 1988, at 58, after a mysterious fall from a third-storey hotel window in Amsterdam.

Theme for Teens

In Vancouver, rock and roll and Red Robinson are synonymous. Over the course of a career that spans half a century, he has introduced radio listeners and concert-goers to countless rock and roll artists and holds the distinction of being one of three Canadian broadcast pioneers inducted into Cleveland, Ohio's Rock and Roll Hall of Fame. Born in Comox on Vancouver Island in 1937, Robinson began spinning discs professionally at 15. Elvis Presley once shackled him to a dressing-room shower stall for amusement and the Beatles' John Lennon told him to "get the fuck off our stage" in the middle of a riot. It has been a remarkable career, to say the least.

"When I was a kid going to high school, I loved music," says Robinson. "I was introduced to it by my mom who, while all the other mothers in the neighbourhood were listening to soap operas on the radio, was listening to music, mostly black artists like Louis Armstrong and Louis Jordan. Consequently, I loved radio and wanted to be on it. Legendary Vancouver broadcaster Jack Cullen was my primary inspiration. He did night shows and I listened to him as a kid. I became myopic; it was all I wanted to do."

One of the highlights in the career of Red Robinson (right foreground) was meeting Elvis Presley in 1957.
Red Robinson Collection

At 15, Robinson began banging on radio-station doors. Due to his lack of experience, however, opportunity wasn't answering. Nonetheless, he persevered. "I guess I'd seen Mickey Rooney and Judy Garland in movies, saying, 'Hey, let's put on a show!' It just seemed to me that nothing was impossible." He was right. After being shown the exit by execs at CJOR, he called the station's afternoon show, the Al Jordan-hosted *Theme for Teens*, and put on a Jimmy Stewart voice. "I knew he was in town," says Robinson, "so I did an impersonation of him, saying, 'Uh, uh, is this Al Jordan? This is Jimmy Stewart and I really love your show.'" Nightlife columnist Jack Wasserman picked up on the story and wrote about it in the *Vancouver Sun*. "Jack said, 'Wasn't that nice of actor Jimmy Stewart to call CJOR's teen show and say hi to the kids?' So I called the station the next day and told them who it really was. After that, they let me start hanging around the studio."

Appreciating that he had to create a niche for himself, Robinson began writing, performing and producing three-minute episodes of a satirical detective series called *Rod Gat*, spoofing Mickey Spillane's Mike Hammer character. "I said things like, 'She lay there in the sun with her blonde hair spilling across the rocks like melted margarine,'" says Robinson, laughing. "It was horrible, *horrible* stuff but it was fun and it drew 1,500 letters a week." When Jordan left the show, Robinson naturally assumed the command post at *Theme for Teens*, often taking it out of CJOR's control room in the Grosvenor Hotel at 840 Howe Street to the station's live radio theatre across the street. "The room held about 120 people," he says. "The kids would come down after school and I'd do the show from there. I had Frankie Laine as a guest, Louis Armstrong—big stars who couldn't perform in the radio theatre because the Musicians Union wouldn't let them but they came and met the kids and I played their records."

The idea proved so successful that lineups for the 4 p.m. show often stretched around the block. When Detroit-born singer Guy Mitchell arrived in town on the heels of his biggest hit, 1956's number one single "Singin' the Blues," Robinson decided to try hosting the show from the Sunset Community Centre. "Guy was in town for two weeks at the Cave," says Robinson. "That's where you got to know these people—when they came in for multiple-night stands. I told him I wanted to do my show from the Sunset and he said, 'Oh, the place that Bing Crosby built?' He already knew that Crosby had performed a benefit concert to raise money for the centre. That show really launched my career. I became like a pied piper. I just had to go everywhere and promote things and I knew I had to do it in front of an audience."

Robinson's next coup was to take *Theme for Teens* to the Kitsilano Showboat. Boogie-woogie pianist Chuck Miller, who'd scored a 1955 hit with "House of Blue Lights," took the Kits Showboat stage and afterwards handed Robinson an acetate by an unknown singer-songwriter from Camus, Washington, named Jimmie Rodgers (not to be confused with "Singing Brakeman" Jimmie Rodgers or Chicago blues artist Jimmy Rogers). "Chuck Miller had just played a club in Vancouver, Washington, called the Frontier and had heard this young man who'd given him an acetate," says Robinson, referring to the vinyl records upstart artists used as demonstration or "demo" recordings. "I put it on and it was 'Honeycomb.' Just Jimmie Rodgers and his guitar. It was the first time anybody'd heard Jimmie Rodgers and the kids loved it." All 10,000 of them, which was the size of the horde at the Kits Showboat that day. "Honeycomb" went on to become one of the biggest-selling records of 1957.

Rodgers would place another 37 songs in the Top 40 over the next decade, including "Kisses Sweeter Than Wine" and "Secretly," before having his skull cracked open by a Los Angeles Police officer in a bizarre incident on the San Diego Freeway in December 1967. The officer claimed Rodgers was drunk and disorderly. It took three surgeries, the insertion of a skull plate and nearly three decades before Rodgers was heard from again. (Unsubstantiated rumours later circulated

Louis Armstrong and *Theme for Teens* host Al Jordan greet young fans in Vancouver. Vancouver Public Library VPL 82431

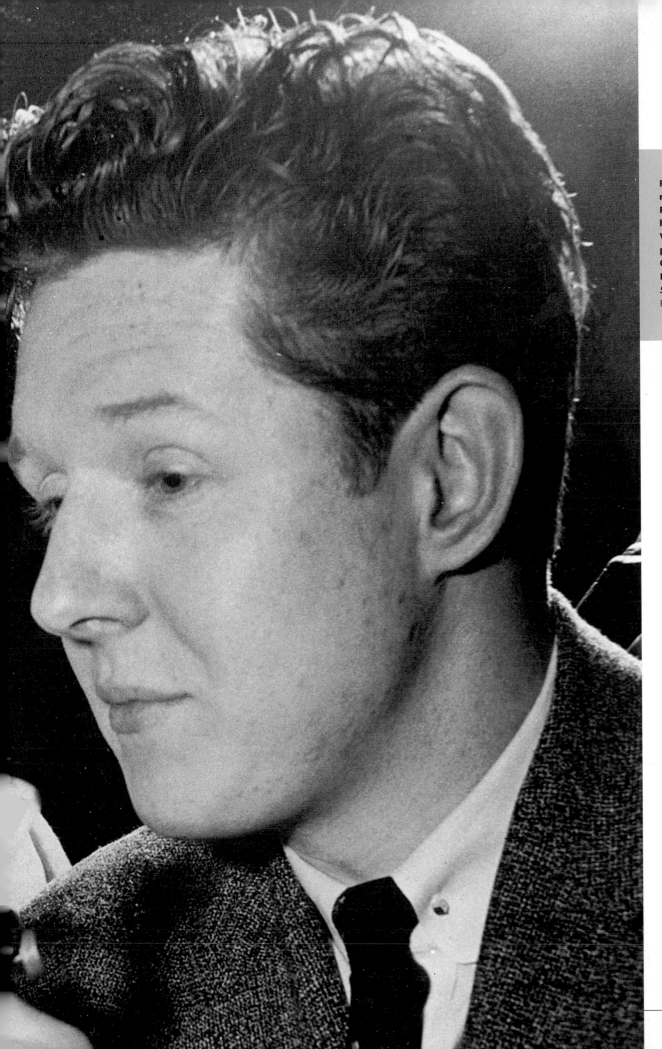

Red enthusiastically promoting Elvis Presley for CJOR at the Kitsilano Showboat.
Red Robinson Collection

Red Robinson works a crowd at the Kitsilano Showboat.
Red Robinson Collection

that Rodgers's record-label boss, upset at his artist's demands for back royalties, paid the cop to shut Rodgers up once and for all.) In an upbeat coda to the tale, Robinson booked Jimmie Rodgers to play Vancouver's Queen Elizabeth Theatre in 1995 as part of Timmy's Telethon, an annual fundraising event mounted by the Lions Society of BC.

"I made a special surprise presentation to Jimmie," says Robinson. "I came onstage and said, 'Jimmie, do you remember Chuck Miller?' And he said, 'How could I forget him? He was the one who got my first record exposed.' I said, 'Do you know what happened to that first record?' He said, 'Oh, it's lost.' I said, 'No, it's not,' and handed him the original acetate. Right there on stage, the man started to cry. He couldn't believe it. He said, 'Ladies and gentlemen, Red has given me the original recording that got me my first record deal.' He was overwhelmed."

Fast-talkin' Red was 15 years old when he began his association with CJOR Radio.
Red Robinson Collection

Rock Around the Clock

Inevitably, the cross-pollination of racially divided musical genres would result in rock and roll, an art form that in its various permutations would either accompany, influence or initiate every major cultural movement for the duration of the 20th century.

Rock and roll arrived in Vancouver on June 27, 1956, when Bill Haley and His Comets took the stage before a crowd of 6,000 at the Kerrisdale Arena. "Jack Cullen brought the group to town and Murray Goldman, the clothier, put up the money," recounts Robinson. "Although Haley didn't record the first rock and roll record, he did record the first one to chart on the *Billboard* pop charts, which was 'Crazy Man Crazy' in 1953. After that came 'Rock Around the Clock,' which hit number one in 1955 and was featured in the movie *Blackboard Jungle* that same year. The following year, a movie called *Rock Around the Clock* was released. Those films were the catalysts that made rock and roll stick. They were big and they were multimedia. Kids were up dancing in the aisles. You actually saw people dancing in movie theatres."

Cullen, whom Robinson characterizes as "a rogue and a rebel but never a bad guy," knew a good thing when he saw it and was prescient enough to realize the Haley show needed an emcee teens could relate to: another teen. "One day I got a call from Jack, who was my competitor," says Robinson, "and he said, 'Red, c'mon down to my studio,' which was in his record store on Hastings and Carrall. We'd both just finished our night shows and it was one o'clock in the morning. He said, 'Murray and I have thought about it and we'd like you to emcee the Bill Haley and His Comets show. We think it's the right thing to do.' Of course, I accepted. It was the first rock and roll concert in the city."

The fact that Haley was a week away from his 31st birthday—ancient from a teenager's perspective—and visibly balding hardly mattered to the crowd, which screamed so loud Robinson was barely able to finish his introduction. Away from the spotlight, however, Haley revealed that matters of age, hipness and relevance were very much on his mind. "That man was so interesting and articulate," says Robinson. "I said to him backstage, 'Bill, it must be fantastic. You're at the top of the world.' He'd just had three Top 20 hits with 'Shake, Rattle and Roll,' 'Rip It Up' and 'Rock Around the Clock.' And he said, 'Well, it's been fun but the ride's over.' I said, 'What do you mean?' After all, this guy was the granddaddy of rock and roll. Sure there was Chuck Berry and Little Richard but it took a white guy to make it happen with the masses. And Haley said, 'There is a very handsome young singer down in Memphis they call 'The Hillbilly Cat.' He's got the looks, he's got the talent and he's young. We're finished.' I thought, man, can this guy predict the future? The concert had been sold out and fans tore the arena apart, throwing chairs everywhere. But Haley himself knew exactly what was going to happen."

Red Robinson emceed the first rock and roll concert held in Vancouver, featuring "Rock Around the Clock" star Bill Haley (right) and His Comets at Kerrisdale Arena, June 27, 1956. Red Robinson Collection

Elvis Presley performing in Vancouver for the one and only time—Empire Stadium, August 31, 1957. Red Robinson Collection

The Hillbilly Cat

Elvis Aron Presley had been born into poverty in East Tupelo, Mississippi, in 1935. Twenty-one years later, he was an international rock and roll star, having wowed television audiences throughout 1956 with appearances on Tommy and Jimmy Dorsey's *Stage Show*, *The Milton Berle Show*, *The Steve Allen Show* and, most famously, *The Ed Sullivan Show*. That same year, every one of his singles, including number-one chart toppers "Heartbreak Hotel," "Hound Dog," "Don't Be Cruel" and "Love Me Tender," was certified gold. The entire world wanted to see the man in the flesh and Vancouverites were no exception. Robinson tried bringing Presley to town, only to be told the singer was tied up working on his third film, *Jailhouse Rock*. "I still have the letter from his manager, Colonel Tom Parker, saying that Elvis wouldn't be in the area," says Robinson.

The following year, however, Presley was going to be in the area and on August 31, 1957, he played his third and final show in Canada—indeed, his third and final show anywhere outside the US—at Empire Stadium. "The man who finally got the tour going was Zollie Volchuck, who owned a promotion company in Seattle called Northwest Releasing," says Robinson. "He worked with Hugh Pickett to bring Elvis to town and they wanted me to emcee it. For me, of course, that was amazing." Unlike the rest of the press corps, the show's promoters, and Robinson, knew that Presley would be arriving by train, not airplane. "The Saturday morning he came to town, everybody in the media was out at the airport," Robinson says with a chuckle. "Meanwhile, I'm out at the old Great Northern train depot at Main and Terminal with Zollie.

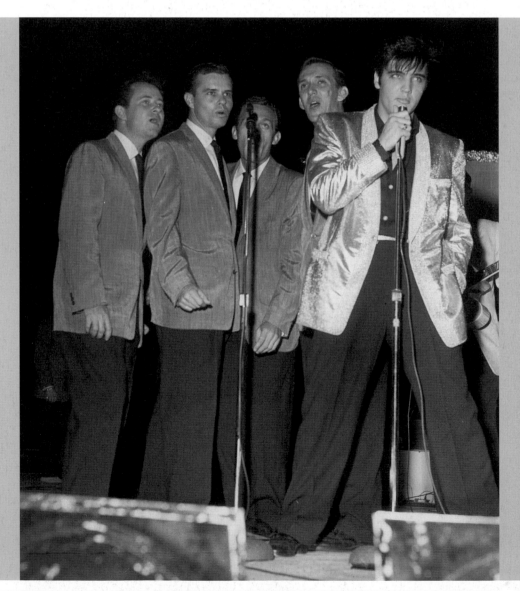

Elvis, Red Robinson points out, was the world's first arena rocker: "Who before Elvis Presley ever rented stadiums? Nobody."
Red Robinson Collection

Opposite: Elvis shakes it up at the Empire Stadium, sending thousands of teenage girls into hysterics.
Red Robinson Collection

"The train stopped just before it got into the station," Robinson continues, "and Elvis got off and walked around a bit. Someone at the railroad must have tipped off somebody else because there were two girls there who'd come down to see him and take some pictures but that was it. From there, we went to the Georgia Hotel and talked for a couple of hours in the afternoon before Elvis had to go out and rehearse. The amazing thing about Presley, Sinatra and other artists of the day is that they sounded exactly like they did on record because they had talent. There was no electronic layering or anything like that.

"He immediately struck me as a very nice, down-to-earth guy. He was about six feet tall and built like an NFL quarterback: a very big, strong guy. There's a picture of the two of us and he is actually kneeling on a bench throughout the entire press conference. He did the whole hour-long interview kneeling on that bench, shifting from one leg to the other. For most people, that would be excruciating, but for him, it was no effort. He also had the biggest hands I've ever seen on anybody. He was just a terrific guy."

After the press conference, Presley and Robinson retired to the BC Lions' dressing room in the pit of Empire Stadium and waited for the show to begin. "We sat back there for about 45 minutes," says Robinson, "and Elvis kept pacing up and down. By that point in my career, I was used to emceeing shows but I was nervous as hell because who before Elvis Presley ever rented stadiums? Nobody. Maybe Bing Crosby or Bob Hope could perform in front of thousands of people, whether for the troops overseas or at big conventions, but nobody ever rented stadiums.

Over the course of a career that spans half a century, Red introduced radio listeners and concert-goers to rock and roll's top artists.
Red Robinson Collection

"So there we are waiting, and Elvis is pacing up and down, and there are just the two of us in the dressing room. Finally he says, 'Red, just wait here for a minute,' and he walks over to the door of the dressing room where two police officers are standing and he says to one of them: 'Excuse me, sir, I'd like to borrow your hat and your badge if I could.' (He was always very polite.) The policeman says, 'Sure.' Then Elvis asks to borrow his handcuffs. The cop says, 'Yeah, okay.' Then he says to me, 'Y'know, Red, we've got all this time. I can see you're nervous and I am, too. Do me a favour and put your arms up over that shower rod there,' and he points to the showers in the Lions' dressing room. Then he starts muttering some gibberish he'd learned for the movie *Jailhouse Rock* and handcuffs me to the shower rod, saying, 'Now you're locked in here,' and throws the key across the concrete floor where I can't see it. This is all fine and dandy—just joking around, right?—but then he starts looking for the key and he can't find it. So he calls in the cop and the two of them are there looking all over the place for the key. After a couple of minutes, Elvis just sort of shrugs and says, 'Gee, Red, we can't seem to find that key anywhere.'

"What's running through my head at this point is, 'Jesus, here I am with the most important star in the world and I'm not going to be able to introduce him because he's got me locked to a shower rod!' Finally, Elvis says, 'Well, I guess I'll have to go introduce myself because you're all tied up.' Then he starts laughing. He'd had the key the whole time. I didn't know it until later but he was a practical joker and used to do things like that all the time. He'd throw ping-pong balls in the swimming pool at Graceland and shoot them with pellet guns. Elvis was really just a big kid. I think that was one of his problems: he never grew up."

A sold-out audience of 25,000 let out a deafening shriek as Robinson introduced Presley. The singer ran from the players' tunnel and hopped into a black Cadillac limousine convertible with the top down to make a slow pass of the stadium perimeter before taking the stage. Dressed in black pants and a black shirt with a gold lamé jacket—the rest of the gilded outfit was too creased and too hot to wear, he told Robinson—Presley ripped the joint, as it were, and the audience followed suit. Escaping at show's end through a trap door in the stage, Presley and Robinson waited beneath the boards while an Elvis stand-in donned the gold-flecked jacket and dashed for the backstage limo. The throng descended on the Elvis impersonator, who narrowly escaped into the players' tunnel.

When the commotion died down and the crowd had dispersed, Presley nonchalantly emerged from his hiding place and climbed into another vehicle for his ride back to the hotel. Robinson returned to the radio station for his 10 p.m. show and at 2:30 a.m., after an evening spent spinning nothing but Presley platters, his private line rang in the studio. It was Elvis personally thanking him and saying goodbye. It was the last time Robinson spoke with the man.

The Show of Stars

In March 1958, Elvis Presley began a two-year hitch in the US Army. Despite the hopes and prayers of elders and detractors, however, rock and roll would not be silenced so easily. That same spring, Ricky Nelson arrived. This was a performer who grew up not only with television but on it, playing himself in his family's series, *The Adventures of Ozzie and Harriet,* from age 12 to 26. The stigma of being "the first teen idol" overshadowed his impressive rockabilly and country recordings and he was often overlooked as a serious musician. He also had the bad luck of playing the PNE Garden Auditorium six months after Presley's electrifying Empire Stadium appearance.

"Right after Elvis, Ricky Nelson came to town," says Robinson, "and even though he had the looks and the music, he didn't have the charisma. He was a real teenager, an idol of the kids and a product of television. As a matter of fact, MTV later gave him the award for having the first music video for 1961's 'Travellin' Man.'

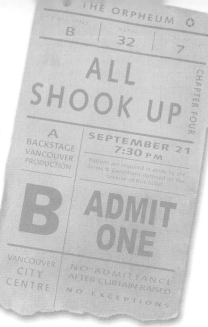

Vancouver fans hoping for a second coming of Elvis ended up booing low-key teen idol Ricky Nelson. Red Robinson Collection

Robinson first met Bobby Darin, creator of "Splish Splash" and "Mack the Knife," during Red's two-year fling at Portland's KGW Radio.
Red Robinson Collection

Rock martyrs: fifteen months after meeting Red at 1957's *Biggest Show of Stars*, 21-year-old Buddy Holly, one of rock's brightest stars, would die in a plane crash. Holly's talented 19-year-old tour-mate Eddie Cochran (opposite right) would die in a car crash shortly after. Red Robinson Collection

But when he played Vancouver, the crowd actually booed him, which was sad. They'd experienced the dynamic of Bill Haley and Elvis, who both shook the stage. They got into it and became whatever the song was. Ricky just stood there like a flashback of Perry Como, except with a guitar and rock and roll music. Between songs, he would go and get a drink of water. Later, he realized what the problem was and changed his stage manner. The funny thing was, people thought he and Elvis were enemies but Ricky wasn't enemies with anybody. In fact, Elvis was a great admirer of Ricky's. The singers and their bands played touch football games together on Saturdays in Los Angeles. The only thing was, though, Elvis had to win."

By the late 1950s, it only made sense that integrated music would give way to integrated bills. Enter Irvin Feld, by no coincidence the owner of the Ringling Bros. Barnum & Bailey Circus. "Feld saw rock and roll as just another carny show," says Robinson, "the same as Colonel Parker. But they realized that this was, indeed, the first explosion of a youth generation. Feld put together *The Show of Stars*, the first rock and roll caravan, and took it all over North America. He had 10 acts on the same bill, so everybody would come out and sing their hit and maybe one other song. You'd have the Everly Brothers, Sam Cooke, Buddy Knox, LaVern Baker, Eddie Cochran, Gene Vincent, Frankie Lymon and the Teenagers, and on and on, one after the other. It was unbelievable—all these people on one package tour. I remember Dave Somerville from the Diamonds—a Toronto vocal group that had hits with 'Why Do Fools Fall in Love' and 'Little Darlin'—telling me about Paul Anka writing a song on the tour bus somewhere in the middle of Canada. The song was 'It Just Doesn't Matter Anymore' and he wrote it for Buddy Holly, who was sitting across the aisle."

Above: Red with Buddy Holly, who said he doubted rock and roll would last past Christmas of 1957.
Red Robinson Collection

Latino star Ritchie Valens, who hit big with "La Bamba" (1959), perished in the same plane crash with Buddy Holly and Big Bopper on "the day the music died," February 3, 1959. When he played Vancouver six weeks earlier, Valens was held up a week because it was too dangerous to fly.
Red Robinson Collection

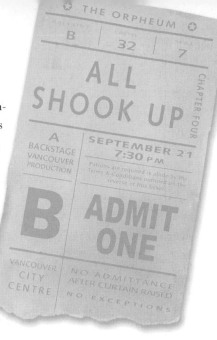

THE ORPHEUM

B 32 7

CHAPTER FOUR

ALL SHOOK UP

A BACKSTAGE VANCOUVER PRODUCTION

SEPTEMBER 21 7:30 PM

Patrons are required to abide by the Terms & Conditions outlined on the reverse of this ticket.

B ADMIT ONE

VANCOUVER CITY CENTRE

NO ADMITTANCE AFTER CURTAIN RAISED NO EXCEPTIONS

Holly, along with Ritchie Valens and the Big Bopper, would die in a much-mythologized plane crash, February 3, 1959. "Today, Buddy Holly is a legend," says Robinson, "but in those days, he was just a kid and I was just a kid. In October 1957, I asked him how long he thought rock and roll was going to be around and he said, 'Maybe until Christmas but not much after that.'" As for Valens, Robinson promoted a pair of Vancouver performances by the Latin-American rocker in 1958. "I booked Ritchie Valens into an old downtown theatre called the International Plaza for a matinee show," he says. "I advertised like crazy but the guy who owned the theatre wouldn't put Ritchie's name on the marquee because he would have had to take down the name of the movie that was playing. Consequently, only about 300 people showed up for the afternoon show. That night, however, 3,000 people turned up at the Cloverdale Arena and Ritchie had to do two shows because they couldn't get all the people into one show.

"It was during the middle of a snowstorm in December," Robinson continues, "and Ritchie couldn't fly out for a week because we had prop planes. Jets didn't come along until 1959 or '60. While he was here, he stayed at the backup band's house. They were called the Stripes and three of them were brothers: Gary O'Bray was the drummer, Garth was a singer and Blaine played bass. Mrs. O'Bray did all the laundry and cooking. Six weeks later, Ritchie Valens was dead. He was 18. When the biopic *La Bamba* came out in 1987, I asked Blaine if he took their mother to see it. He said, 'Yes, and she cried all the way through. It brought back all those memories of a young man who was a star for maybe a year.'"

The Everly Brothers played with Buddy Holly, Eddie Cochran and others in *The Biggest Show of Stars* at the Georgia Auditorium, October 23, 1957. Red Robinson Collection

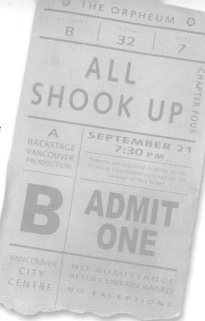

The Platinum Blondes

Musical artists, of course, weren't the only ones to pass through town during the 1950s. The decade was memorably bracketed by the arrival of Marilyn Monroe, who stayed for five minutes in 1952 (but returned shortly after on a promotional junket for *Gentlemen Prefer Blondes*), and Errol Flynn, who arrived in the autumn of 1959 and left six days later in a plain pine box. Monroe's harried and breathless stopover was captured on tape by Jack Cullen as she hobbled across the tarmac at Vancouver International Airport on a pair of crutches (she had broken her ankle in Banff while filming *River of No Return* with Robert Mitchum):

Jack Cullen: Ladies and gentlemen, this promises to be perhaps one of the quickest interviews we've done on this program. We greet you from the International Airport. So with no further ado, let's find out what brings Marilyn Monroe back to Vancouver.

Marilyn Monroe: Hello, Jack. Well, it's wonderful to be back here. I love it here in Vancouver but it's just for a brief visit. I'm just in between planes.

Opposite: If you've got it, flaunt it. Marilyn Monroe earns the devotion of forklift operators the world over at Vancouver International Airport, 1952. Vancouver Public Library VPL 62485 *The Province*

Marilyn Monroe talks to deejays Dowin Baird (l) and Monty McFarlane (r) during a stop in Vancouver to promote *Gentlemen Prefer Blondes*. Monty McFarlane Collection

JC: How do you feel with this game leg you're sporting?

MM: Well, it's much better now. I broke a ligament about two weeks ago but it's better. I think I'll have to be on my crutches for, oh, another two or three weeks and I'll be all right.

JC: *River of No Return* is the picture you just finished. Is that right?

MM: Yes, well, we're just finishing it. We have a little bit to do back in Hollywood.

JC: We happen to know that *Gentlemen Prefer Blondes* is opening in Vancouver at Ivan Ackery's Orpheum Theatre. He wants a big send-off. What do you hear about the picture? How is it being received?

MM: Oh, wonderful. I'm so happy it's going to open here. Well, of course, so far from the studio, I've just heard reports that it's been going very well and I'm very thrilled about it. You don't know what it means to me and the rest of the people in the picture, Jane Russell included.

JC: Also, very briefly, we'd like to ask: What are Marilyn Monroe's future plans when she gets back down south?

MM: Well, uh, to finish this picture and then there are plans to go to Korea, which I'm looking forward to very much, even though, uh, with the troops, you know. They still need entertainment very badly over there.

JC: How long will it be before you're going to be well?

MM: Well, I think it's going to be another two or three more weeks until I'm over it.

JC: You better take it easy. I know you're in a hurry to catch the plan. We just want to say, thanks a million.

MM: I have to run, now, Jack, 'cause they're yelling.

JC: Nice to have met you. Really.

MM: Thanks a million to you and the people of Vancouver.

JC: Okay.

MM: Bye-bye.

JC: Well, at least we've met Marilyn Monroe and that's half the battle.

If the other half of the battle was meeting Jayne Mansfield, the so-called "poor man's Marilyn Monroe," CBC theatre critic Ben Metcalf did just that in the late 1950s, when Mansfield brought her nightclub routine to Vancouver. Despite speaking five languages, boasting an IQ of 163 and being a classically trained pianist and violinist, the busty actress was repeatedly saddled with roles that accentuated her natural wonders—self-described as 44D-18-36—rather than her acting. Her career in decline, she launched a self-parodying nightclub act.

According to Metcalf, Mansfield and second husband Mickey Hargitay were attending a soirée in the Hotel Vancouver ballroom at which Burrard Band Native leader Chief Dan George also happened to be present. "I've never had a chief before," Mansfield reportedly remarked to no one in particular, and excusing herself from Hargitay, who was evidently quite used to this sort of behaviour, took George by the arm and led him upstairs.

The Long, Slow Death of Captain Blood

The curtain came down on Tasmanian-born screen idol Errol Flynn during a 1959 visit to Vancouver to negotiate the sale of his yacht, the *Zaca,* to local businessman George Caldough. News agencies from around the world descended on the city and covered the story enthusiastically, if not always accurately. Flynn, born in 1909, had been the suave and handsome star of early action flicks *Captain Blood*, *The Charge of the Light Brigade*, *The Adventures of Robin Hood*, *The Dawn Patrol*, *They Died With Their Boots On* and *Gentleman Jim* (all filmed between 1935 and 1942). By the time he turned up in Vancouver, however, the 50-year-old Flynn's excessive lifestyle had rendered him alcoholic, virtually penniless and "with the body of an 80-year-old man."

It has been opined that Flynn, still recovering from the financial walloping of one statutory rape acquittal, was likely fleeing from another. In fact, his 17-year-old "protegé" of two years, Beverly Aadland, accompanied him to the city even though he was still married to his third wife, B-film actress Patrice Wymore. Upon arrival at Vancouver International Airport, *Vancouver Sun* reporter Ruth Pinkus asked Flynn why he always seemed to be accompanied by young girls. Neither Flynn nor Aadland so much as batted an eye when the actor shot back, "Because they fuck so good!" *Sun* nightlife columnist Jack Wasserman was horrified and swore he'd never mention Errol Flynn's name in his column again. The events of a few days later quickly changed his mind.

This much is known: Flynn and Aadland flew into town October 9, 1959. On October 14, Caldough and his wife were taking the pair to the airport for a return flight to Los Angeles when Flynn, who'd been feeling ill for several days, asked for a doctor. Caldough immediately changed course for the Sylvia Hotel on English Bay to locate the house doctor, Grant Gould (cousin of acclaimed Canadian pianist Glenn Gould). After being informed that he wasn't there, Caldough called Gould's office and the doctor suggested they meet at his apartment at 1310 Burnaby Street in the city's West End. In a somewhat peculiar turn of events, the checkup turned into a party with booze flowing freely and Flynn holding court, doing imitations of Bette Davis, John Barrymore and W.C. Fields.

The alcohol, however, wasn't alleviating Flynn's discomfort and he complained of severe back pain, finally excusing himself to lie on the floor of Dr. Gould's bedroom. Aadland looked in on him half an hour later and discovered that Flynn had turned blue and his lips were trembling. He was unable to form words and Aadland, by all accounts mature and sensible despite her age and lifestyle choice, performed mouth-to-mouth in a vain attempt to resuscitate the actor. Dr. Gould and Caldough also attempted to revive Flynn by thumping on his chest. An ambulance and fire department inhalator were summoned but Dr. Gould had already pronounced Flynn dead at 6:35 p.m. The ambulance took the body to Vancouver General Hospital, where he was once again pronounced dead.

On the run from various legal, financial and personal problems, action adventure star Errol Flynn's initial reason for coming to Vancouver in 1959 was to sell his yacht. Deni Eagland *Vancouver Sun*

According to Judge Glen McDonald of Vancouver's Coroner's Court (in his 1984 autobiography *How Come I'm Dead?*), the body was then chauffeured up the back alley of Skid Row's Cordova Street to the Coroner's Court. After checking for a pulse and conducting a "violent stimulation of the soles of the feet" (routine examinations) McDonald pronounced Errol Flynn dead for a third time. The fun, it seems, was just beginning.

As reporters and cameramen besieged the office, foreign correspondents tied up the coroner's phone lines. The name "E. FLYNN" had been written on the morgue's chalkboard and, as the story goes, a cardboard tent card of the sort used to reserve restaurant tables was set on the autopsy slab, reading, "Mr. Flynn, your table is ready." The body was stripped and Flynn's meagre belongings—$79.70 in cash, a credit card, a cigarette lighter, a "cheap-looking" ring and a gold watch inscribed with the initials "E.F."—were itemized. His toe was tagged, identifying the body, and a grease pencil used to mark his thigh with his name and morgue number. According to McDonald, "His face was sallow and a bit puffy and he looked an awful lot older than 50 years. He looked worn out, wasted." The autopsy concluded that the death was due to "natural causes," including "myocardial infarction, coronary thrombosis, coronary atherosclerosis, fatty degeneration of the liver, portal cirrhosis of the liver and diverticulosis of the colon." In other words, Flynn had been in mighty rough shape.

Perhaps strangest of all the weird events surrounding Flynn's demise was the deep fascination chief pathologist Dr. Tom Harmon held for the prodigious size and number of venereal warts ringing the end of the swashbuckler's well-worn penis. Despite McDonald's objections—"How can we send Mr. Flynn back to his wife with part of his bloody endowment missing?"—Harmon took the liberty of removing the warts and placing them in a jar of formaldehyde. When McDonald returned to the autopsy room, it was the first thing he noticed. Fearing the publicity and lawsuits inherent in such a move, he demanded of Harmon, "Did Errol Flynn expire because he had warts on his dong?" The two of them were howling with laughter by this point. In a burst of inspiration that lent a crowning glory to the already surreal affair, the judge and doctor removed the warts from the formaldehyde and attached them back on the penis—with scotch tape.

"I stuck them back where they belonged," McDonald recalled. "And I was relieved to learn later, talking with the Chief Coroner in Los Angeles, that a further autopsy was performed and the results concurred in every respect with what we had found. The scotch tape was never mentioned. Odd, that. I thought somebody down there would have noticed."

BACKSTAGE VANCOUVER

Vancouver's "Hippie Hollow," a cubbyhole of countercultural activity situated around Kitsilano's West Fourth Avenue, flourished as the epicentre for high times during the late 1960s and 1970s. A mirror image of San Francisco's Haight-Ashbury district, the area blossomed with communes, head shops and hangouts, attracting not only thousands of young Canadians from across the country but scores of young Americans dodging the Vietnam draft. Protests and "Be-Ins" (outdoor music and arts fairs) were mounted with zeal and the seeds of what would become BC's cash-crop marijuana industry were quite literally sown. Forever after, the West Coast would be synonymous with the term "laid back."

In showbiz, however, old-school headliners and hardliners held on and the boundaries between the Freaks and the Establishment were clearly drawn. The division was most evident on the city's bustling and neon-lit Hornby Street, a strip of cocktail lounges and showroom cabarets featuring the Cave Supper Club, arguably the hottest—and certainly the tackiest—of the lot. Located in the 600-block between Georgia and Dunsmuir, the club's interior indeed resembled a subterranean cavern, complete with plaster stalactites hanging from the ceiling. Bette Midler remarked on them, during a visit early in her career. "The first thing she did when she walked out," recounts Hugh Pickett, "was lay down on the stage, look up at the ceiling and say 'I don't think the man who invented stucco really meant for this to happen.'"

You'd never know it today, but in 1948 Vancouver's Hornby Street was a lively neon strip of popular night-clubs such as the Cave, located between Georgia and Dunsmuir. City of Vancouver Archives CVA 1184-3470

THE ORPHEUM

B | 32 | 7

CHAPTER FIVE

SOMETHING
IN
THE AIR

A
BACKSTAGE
VANCOUVER
PRODUCTION

SEPTEMBER 21
7:30 PM

Patrons are required to abide by the
Terms & Conditions outlined on the
reverse of this ticket

B ADMIT
ONE

VANCOUVER
CITY
CENTRE

NO ADMITTANCE
AFTER CURTAIN RAISED
NO EXCEPTIONS

The Cave was a home-away-from-home for entertainers such as Duke Ellington, Buddy Rich, Sammy Davis Jr., Milton Berle, Dan Rowan and Dick Martin, Liza Minnelli, Wayne Newton, Pearl Bailey and Johnny Rivers, to name a handful. It wouldn't have been unusual to see cracker-barrel comedian George Gobel, with his cropped blond brush cut and black-tie tux, vacating the dressing room while the addled and unwashed Eric Burdon and the Animals waited to pour in. Ginger Rogers regularly worked the Cave crowd from the 1940s through to the 1970s. Ella Fitzgerald recorded a live album there on May 19, 1968, with an ensemble headed by saxophonist Fraser McPherson, who led the house band from 1964 to 1970. Every June, without fail, Mitzi Gaynor booked the room for a two-week stretch to debut her latest Las Vegas routine.

"It was an awful place," Gaynor remarked, only half-joking, two decades after the club's extinction in 1981. "It was ugly and looked like it hadn't been cleaned in about 500 years, but it always sold out. They had people standing outside offering the cashiers $100 bills just for a standing-room ticket." One eventful evening, a crowd of loggers jammed the Cave to catch Gaynor's 9 p.m. dinner show. Moments into her closing number, "You Are the Sunshine of My

A skipping unicyclist was among the diverse lineup of acts that could be seen at the Cave Supper Club (note the plaster stalactites). Vancouver Public Library VPL 40652 *The Province*

Jazz percussionist Lionel Hampton, "The King of the Vibes" (right), clowns it up with Dal Richards at the Cave. Dal Richards Collection

Opposite: *South Pacific* star Mitzi Gaynor found Vancouver's Cave a good tryout venue for her Las Vegas revues until her act was broken up by rowdy loggers.

Life," fisticuffs erupted and brawls broke out all over the club. One combatant was hurled from the balcony and landed on a ground-floor table, his fall broken by other people's dinners and drinks. Gaynor quickly regained control of the crowd, only to lose it again. "I said, 'Just a minute, please! Whaddya think I am? Klondike Annie for Heaven's sake? This isn't the Yukon! Just sit down and shut up.' I had about three minutes to go. Well, they sat back down and quieted but as soon as the band started up again: BANG! The fights started up all over and this time they spilled out into the street. I finished the last high note and said, 'I'll see you guys later.'"

The Saloon Beat

"My favourite story from the Cave Supper Club," says former *Vancouver Sun* columnist Denny Boyd, "goes back to when Fraser McPherson was leading the house orchestra in the 1960s. Fraser was very sophisticated and an absolutely superb musician but he was a strange guy to be a jazz musician. He read poetry and great books. To be making his living leading a band in a nightclub always seemed to me to be below him. He never fell into that whole jazz lifestyle. When the band had a break, they would go upstairs to the dressing room where sidemen like trumpet player Stew Barnett or bassist Cuddles Johnston would scuttle to their lockers and break out the Beefeater gin. But Fraser wouldn't even have to pour a drink. The Cave management knew the moment they saw him heading backstage to rush his favourite brandy or port up to him in a little snifter."

Boyd, who was called up from the sports desk to replace *Vancouver Sun* saloon columnist Jack Wasserman after the latter had run afoul of the paper's management, recalls an especially touchy situation that occurred when African-American singer Lou Rawls was booked into the club. "Rawls received a crude letter," says Boyd. "It was a Ku Klux Klan handbill warning him that he'd 'better be out of town by sundown or he'd get his black head blown off.' That night, while Rawls was singing, a waitress told Dave Davie, the Cave's 275-pound backstage-security bouncer and a one-time sparring partner for fifties heavyweight champ Rocky Marciano, that there was an owly-looking man in the audience who appeared to be holding a gun under his table.

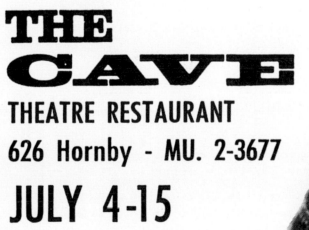

Star
of the film
South Pacific and
countless T.V. shows . . .

Mitzi Gaynor

brings her vital personality,
her versatile talents and
her own review to
the stage of

THE
CAVE

THEATRE RESTAURANT
626 Hornby - MU. 2-3677

JULY 4-15

A death threat from the Ku Klux Klan couldn't stop "pre-rap" singer Lou Rawls from performing at the Cave, even after the bouncer had to tackle a gun-toting audience member.
Peter Hulbert *Vancouver Sun*

Opposite: Lou Rawls' distinctive singing voice was said to be "sweet as sugar, soft as velvet, strong as steel, smooth as butter."
Ian Lindsay *Vancouver Sun*

"Now, Davie had just come out of the hospital after surgery that required opening up his ribs," Boyd continues. "The suspected gunman's table had a waist-high, wrought-iron partition in front but Davie figured he could go over headfirst and grab the guy's right hand without hurting his own tender ribs. That's how he timed it, and just as he went over the rail, the guy brought the gun up—in his left hand. But Big Dave was quick. He hit the table, rolled and smothered the gun, while almost passing out from the pain. It turned out the gun wasn't loaded. The weirdo was hustled away by the police and driven to the US border. But Davie never got over Rawls's reaction: the singer raised hell about the commotion, but when the circumstances were explained to him, he didn't even thank Dave."

Gunplay also figured into an incident involving acerbic New York comedian Jack "Funnyman" Carter. "Jack Carter was a very irreverent and tough-talking guy," says Boyd. "He was known for his abrasive wit but, evidently, one night he went too far because somebody was trying to kill him." Indeed, directly across the street from the Cave, Carter was pinned down on the sidewalk on his hands and knees in the pouring rain while a car drove past, firing live rounds of ammunition at the entertainer. "They were most certainly trying to hit him," says Boyd, "but they missed.'"

A considerably less lethal, though equally intense, situation erupted one evening when Cave staff member Joe "Two-fer" Freeman inadvertently caused hearts to skip a beat. "The Cave employed Joe 'Two-fer' to walk around

The Penthouse was a long-serving after-hours club frequented by stars and hookers. Its irrepressible owner Joe Philliponi was gunned down in a gangland-style killing in 1983. John Denniston *The Province*

town passing out complimentary two-for-one tickets to people on the street whenever a show wasn't selling," remembers Boyd. "But he was also the club's lighting man and he had a little booth up in the balcony, where he handled all the lights." One week the McGuire Sisters—Phyllis, Dorothy and Christine—were booked to play the club. Before the set, lead singer Phyllis was seated at a large table with her boyfriend at the time, infamous Chicago crime boss Sam Giancana, and "three or four guys with very big shoulders." Suddenly, a sound like a shotgun blast rang out: the result of Freeman having accidentally dropped a globe light that exploded with a sharp report. "The next thing you knew," Boyd cackles, "Sam and Phyllis were sitting all by themselves because the bodyguards were hiding under the table."

Meanwhile, Basil Pantages had built a club of his own across the street from the Cave. "Basil was the nephew of Alexander Pantages, founder of the famous theatre circuit and one of the more prominent guys around town," says Boyd. "When Basil opened his place, he invited Penthouse Cabaret owner Joe Philliponi to be his guest. Basil started bragging to Joe that he had a machine that made the 'best ice cubes in the business. I keep them iced down to serve with the setups.' The 'setup' was a glass, a bowl of ice cubes and whatever mixer you'd asked for. Joe, who always said everything twice, looked at Basil and said, 'Kid, kid. Now listen to me, listen

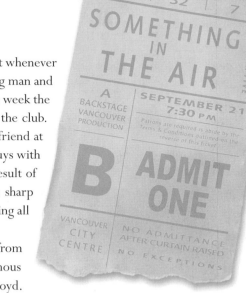

Before getting busted as a common bawdy house in 1976, the Penthouse offered wholesome entertainment from the likes of Harry Belafonte, Ella Fitzgerald and Sammy Davis Jr.
Vancouver Public Library
VPL 53715

to me. You wanna sell ice cubes? You don't keep 'em in the fridge; you keep 'em on top of the stove. That way, the customers gotta keep ordering ice cubes because the ones they got are melting as soon as they hit the table.'"

Sometime later, Pantages stood on Hornby Street watching his dream go up in flames. "One night, the place caught on fire," says Boyd. "Wasserman heard about it and headed down. There, he ran into Basil and they're standing on the sidewalk side by side. Jack saw that Basil was weeping, tears just flowing down his face. Jack said, 'Don't worry, Baz. The insurance will cover everything.' Basil turned to Jack and said, 'I don't have any insurance.' A couple of minutes later, Pantages looked to his side and tears were running down Wasserman's face. Jack felt so sorry for him."

Nightclub owner Joe Philliponi warrants mention of his own establishment. "You can't talk about Vancouver nightlife without talking about the Penthouse," says Boyd. "The Penthouse was originally a bottle club, an after-hours place. If, for example, a nightclub comedian finished up at one or two o'clock in the morning, they could go to the Penthouse, get a bottle of bootleg hooch and a pretty good steak. Plus, the Penthouse had the first authentic pizza oven in Vancouver, imported piece by piece from Italy. Sammy Davis Jr., Frank Sinatra, Lena Horne, Mitzi Gaynor, just about everybody went there at one time or another. They had a musical combo in there and it was a place where you could sit with your cronies—club owners, restaurant owners, people in the same business as you—have a bite to eat and have a bottle that you kept under the table.

"The Penthouse occupied a rather interesting function in Vancouver," Boyd continues. "All of the hookers, rather than standing on street corners, hung out at the Penthouse. Guys from judges to thugs knew they could go to the Penthouse and meet a nice, clean hooker. It kept the girls off the street but it drove the goddamn vice squad crazy. The silly bastards just kept raiding the place until they threw the hookers back onto the street. I remember, one time, somebody was interviewing Joe Philliponi and the matter of the Penthouse's morality came into question. Joe said, 'Listen to me, listen to me! I ain't Rebecca and this ain't Sunnybrook Farm!'" Philliponi ran the club until

Vancouver Sun columnist Jack Wasserman delighted in the role of man-about-town until the frenetic lifestyle felled him with a heart attack at age 50 in 1977.
Vancouver Public Library VPL 80377

he was murdered on his own premises, execution-style, in 1983. "By that time," says Boyd, "the hookers were gone, and out of desperation, the club started bringing in strippers."

When it came to the saloon-column beat, Boyd confesses, "I didn't really enjoy doing it. I didn't want to be famous. I didn't want to be 'Mr. Vancouver.' I just wanted to go write my column and use good words. The biggest pitfall was the booze; everybody wanted to buy you drinks. The club owners expected you to be there at ringside for opening nights and the drinks were always free. And there were no shifts to speak of; I was on my own, as was Jack. We didn't keep any kind of regular hours, as long as we got back to the office sober enough to write a column—which I occasionally did not do. That beat certainly didn't do anything for my ego, though it sustained Jack's ego."

For a time, that is. Undoubtedly due in part to the lifestyle, Jack Wasserman died at 50, of a heart attack on April 6, 1977, while speaking at a celebrity roast for "Bull of the Woods" logger, politician and millionaire Gordon Gibson at the Hotel Vancouver. "He suddenly just pitched forward into the microphone, bounced off the dais and was dead by the time he hit the floor," says Boyd. Hornby Street was later consecrated "Wasserman's Beat" in his honour. In Vancouver, the saloon column died with him, replaced by a legion of workaday entertainment reporters.

The British Invasion

"In the early sixties," says Vancouver-based rock mogul Bruce Allen, "the premier booking agency in the city was Jaguar Enterprises, which was controlled by Les Vogt [one of the town's earliest rock and roll singers] and Douglas Miller [later a local TV weatherman; later still, the mayor of Lions Bay]. There was a big club scene here at

Five Man Cargo was one of Vancouver's all-time favourite cover bands. They also played an important role in preparing the city for the British Invasion.
Deni Eagland *Vancouver Sun*

Opening question of the Beatles' Vancouver Press Conference: "We heard reports that... they wouldn't let [you] into Canada. Why?" John: "Because of the hair. Have to be deloused before you can get in." Red Robinson Collection

the time and those guys controlled almost all the clubs. It was really funny because the bands were basically R&B acts with white guys playing music behind black frontmen. Then music started to switch a bit more to the Beatles and that type stuff."

A rhythm-and-blues fanatic working at Canadian Kenworth building truck cabs, Allen was drawn into the music business by a partner of ex-BC Lion Bill Lasseter, who ran a club at Broadway and Victoria known as Lasseter's Den. Allen was convinced to help out a hot new group of Hong Kong ex-pats subsequently christened Five Man Cargo, whom he proceeded to equip with lights, stage outfits and a regular gig playing "English music" at Lasseter's club. Astutely capitalizing on the British Invasion of the early sixties, Allen's endeavour spearheaded a Vancouver cover-band craze that encouraged working musicians to hone their chops at nightclubs, high school dances and university frat parties well into the eighties.

After giving Drew Burns's Fifth Day Club—held in large ballrooms at the Hotel Vancouver and Georgia Hotel—its largest crowd ever, Five Man Cargo became in high demand at fiercely competitive downtown hotspots such as Oil Can Harry's, Pharoah's and the Marco Polo. Allen increasingly had to find suitable replacement bands and quickly realized that if he secured a monopoly on nightclub bookings his bands would make more money. "There is a point where the club is happy to pay you and the band is making enough money," says Allen. "It's all changed. In fact, it's ass-backwards now and bands virtually pay to play these days. But back then, the clubs were

happy to pay the bands, the bands were thrilled to be working five or six nights a week and everybody was making money. They called it 'management,'" he says with a smirk, "but I was really just a booking agent."

By the time the genuine British acts transported their revved-up renditions of American blues and R&B back across the Atlantic, North Americans were well aware of what to expect and were waiting with open arms. And thanks to the powerful new publicity tool of television, these acts wouldn't be playing nightclubs.

On Saturday, August 22, 1964, chart-topping British quartet the Beatles made their first and last Vancouver appearance, at Empire Stadium. The previous April, they'd miraculously held the top five spots on *Billboard*'s singles chart with "Can't Buy Me Love," "Twist and Shout," "She Loves You," "I Want to Hold Your Hand" and "Please Please Me." Although it had been seven years since Elvis Presley's Empire Stadium performance culminated in a melee, apparently the cops, city fathers and local promoters had learned nothing about crowd control.

"Here we had another occasion where the crowd crushed towards the front of the stage and all hell broke loose,"

On August 22, 1964, John Lennon and the Beatles precipitated a melee at Empire Stadium.
Red Robinson Collection

says Red Robinson, who was once again handed the emceeing chores (after fellow broadcaster Fred Latremouille came down with mononucleosis). "They didn't learn from the Elvis debacle that, when you have a concert in a stadium, you have to sell tickets on the field so that people aren't leaping out of the stands from the 50-yard line and rushing forward because they've paid for their ticket and they want to see the show. They sold about 25,000 tickets for that concert, and you gotta remember, in those days they didn't have big stacks of amplifiers and towers of sound equipment like they have now. The band just had these little Vox guitar amplifiers and a PA system without any monitors."

The only discernible difference between the donnybrook at the Presley concert and the one shaping up on that August afternoon was the number of security personnel present—not to save the fans from themselves but to save the band from its fans. "It was the first time I ever saw what they call 'gatekeepers,'" says Robinson. "They had trailers backstage for the musicians and bodyguards were stationed outside. Nobody got in to see the band. When guys like Buddy Holly or Sam Cooke or Eddie Cochran had come to town a few years earlier, they'd say after the show, 'Where do we go now?' And I'd say, 'Let's go to the White Spot and have a hamburger,' and we'd go over there and sit down and eat. But that was in 1957. Things had changed."

After the press conference held for the band's arrival, Robinson chinwagged with John, Paul, George and Ringo

One reason fans rushed the Beatles' stage was that they couldn't hear—the band's little guitar amplifiers were too weak for the big football stadium. Red Robinson Collection – Harold Coppin

THE ORPHEUM

B 32 7

CHAPTER FIVE

SOMETHING IN THE AIR

A BACKSTAGE VANCOUVER PRODUCTION

SEPTEMBER 21 7:30 PM

Patrons are required to abide by the terms & conditions outlined on the reverse of this ticket

B ADMIT ONE

VANCOUVER CITY CENTRE

NO ADMITTANCE AFTER CURTAIN RAISED

NO EXCEPTIONS

as he would with any group of visiting hitmakers, but when it was time to go to the stadium, protocol altered dramatically. "I was right behind the stage where the Beatles' trailer was parked," says Robinson. "Jackie DeShannon, the Righteous Brothers, the Exciters and Bill Black's Combo (Black had been Elvis's bass player in '57) were the warm-up acts and they were already taking the stage in quick succession. I'd been talking with the Beatles backstage and they all knew who I was, but when they went into the trailer, the bodyguard outside wouldn't let me past.

"So finally I said to this guy, 'Will you just do me one goddamn favour? Will you just give this photograph to John Lennon? He specifically asked for it.' Within seconds, the trailer door flies open and it's Lennon. He says, 'C'mon in here. I didn't know you were out here.' And to the bodyguard he says, 'Why'd you hold this man up waiting out here?' What I'd given the bodyguard to show Lennon was a picture of me and Buddy Holly. Lennon said, 'I just want to know more about this picture.' So I went inside and sat down and told him about Buddy Holly. I said, 'He was just a guy, a kid really, but he was an innovator and he was prepared to do whatever came along because he wanted to stay in show business.' Then I played the tape of my Buddy Holly interview for John Lennon, the one in which Holly predicted rock and roll wouldn't last past Christmas 1957. Lennon just looked at me and said, 'Yup, and they make us out to be something we're not.'"

Robinson's encounter with Lennon didn't end there. When it came time to introduce the band, the crowd situation had gone from bad to worse. "The kids started pouring down from the stands and onto the field," says Robinson, "and the only guards—Boy Scouts and Air Cadets, who were kids, too—were at the front of the stage. The thrust of kids pushing against the stage made Beatles' manager Brian Epstein more panicky than the Vancouver police chief, who was standing there with us. Epstein, who was used to soccer crushes in England, realized—which we didn't—how easily a person can be suffocated or trampled in a mob like that. He said, 'We've got to get up there right now and stop the show.' I said, 'No way. I'm not going to interrupt their act.' Then the police chief said to me, 'I'm ordering you up there to stop this show. You get on that stage and tell the kids to quiet down or the Beatles are not going to perform.'

"So I get up there and I'm trying to quiet down the crowd and suddenly behind my shoulder, over the cacophony of the crowd, I hear John Lennon yelling at me, 'Get the fuck off our stage! What the fuck are you doing on our stage? Nobody interrupts a Beatles' performance!' There's a photograph where I'm talking to John, actually screaming at him over the roar of the crowd, and I said, 'John, look down at the edge of the stage. Do you think I want to be up here? Your boss and the chief of police ordered me up here to try and settle down the crowd.' At that point he said, 'Oh, in that case, carry on, mate. But no one has ever done this before. There's never been a need.'" Epstein mounted the shaky makeshift platform and had a word with Paul McCartney, who politely asked the audience to pipe down. "They played one more song," says Robinson, "and got the hell out of there."

The following day, Jack Wasserman reported, "The Beatles were onstage for a total of 29 minutes and 23 seconds. It took 35 minutes for the welcoming screams to die down enough for them to start." Although Lennon later apologized to Robinson for his outburst, the deejay's opinion of the star's personality, though not his talent, had soured. "You have to remember that John Lennon wasn't always the nicest guy," Robinson emphasizes. "Out of all the Beatles, he could be really nasty and really mean. He struck me as arrogant and pompous. He appeared to consider himself far above his peers and seemed to enjoy the inevitable media putdowns more than the other three. In my opinion, he saw himself as a clever intellectual. Now, that doesn't take away from his talent or creativity but he just wasn't a sweetheart of a guy. But he really loved Buddy Holly."

Got Live If You Want It

In 1965, a whole new kind of entertainment assaulted Vancouver in the form of the Rolling Stones. The shabbily dressed and ill-kempt quintet—vocalist Mick Jagger, guitarists Keith Richards and Brian Jones, bassist Bill Wyman and drummer Charlie Watts—performed in the city for the first time at the PNE Agrodome, December 1, 1965.

Opposite: Mick Jagger belts it out at the Rolling Stones' first appearance at the Vancouver Agrodome in 1965. Robinson remembers Mick Jagger as "downright offensive." Dee Lippingwell

Robinson's backstage impression of the Stones—shown here at a return engagement in 1981: "Without a doubt the ugliest bunch of guys I'd ever seen, and they were all tiny." Dee Lippingwell

The band, in collusion with its imaginative and media-savvy manager/producer Andrew Loog Oldham, mounted a calculated counteroffensive on the Beatles' clean-cut image. In doing so, they set a standard for arrogance, aloofness and obnoxiousness it would take 10 years and the Sex Pistols to surpass.

Given the impact of AM radio in the mid-1960s, it is not surprising that the city's top pop stations, CFUN and CKLG, bid ferociously for concert and in-person promotional rights. When the 'LG crew got wind that CFUN had hired two limousines to greet the Stones at Vancouver International Airport and transport them downtown to a pre-arranged press conference, the latter station struck back by hiring three limos and dispatching them simultaneously. Airport security being somewhat lax in those days, all five vehicles jockeyed for position on the tarmac in front of the Stones' private jet. Jagger and his bodyguard landed in a limo with CKLG reporters, while his bandmates ducked into cars hired by CFUN, the rightful promoters. Robinson, who worked for CFUN at the time, watched the carnival from the airport lounge "not realizing that CKLG was pulling a fast one on the ramp downstairs." In fact, he says, his first inkling that things had run amok came fast and hard.

"I wouldn't have questioned anything at all," he says, "except that, as usual, I was monitoring the competition to find out what they were playing at that hour. That's when I heard one of the 'LG announcers say, 'And now, live from the airport, the first exclusive Vancouver interview with the Rolling Stones!' There was a commotion on the air and then I heard, as did all of CKLG's listeners, an unmistakable voice with a British accent very clearly demanding, 'What the fuck do you think you're doing? I said NO BLOODY MICROPHONES!'" The next sound was that of a car door opening as Jagger's bodyguard heaved 'LG's broadcasters out of the limousine.

"Later on, we went backstage and there were two things I couldn't get over," Robinson remembers. "They were without a doubt the ugliest bunch of guys I'd ever seen and they were all tiny—about five-foot-seven or five-foot-eight. After what had happened with the Beatles, I said to Fred [Latremouille], 'You introduce them.' So we go backstage to interview them and Mick Jagger says, 'I don't know if I want to talk to any of you or not.' It was the first time in my career, in any of our careers, that we'd ever come across an ornery artist. John Lennon may have been combative and condescending but Mick Jagger was downright offensive and unco-operative. 'Naw, I don't want to talk to anybody,' Jagger kept saying. 'I don't know whether I should or not. Anybody got a cigarette? Anybody got a fag?' He was just completely nasty to everybody.

"I thought, 'Wow, this is a whole new thing,'" Robinson continues. "Jagger took the rebel-without-a-cause *Wild One*-persona to a whole new level. I remember looking over at this little punk and thinking, 'What the hell's he doing?' Remember, the Rolling Stones were a new band and needed the backup of North American radio stations, especially in a major market such as Vancouver. I'm not knocking the band's music or success—and they've certainly espoused those attitudes their entire career—but at the time, it was crazy. Jagger may have improved over the years but he left many disenchanted people in Vancouver after that first visit. Artists just didn't behave that way."

The Rolling Stones returned to Vancouver the following summer and played the PNE Forum on July 19, 1966. According to a Canadian Press newspaper account, "Thirty-six teenagers were carried from an auditorium here Tuesday after a disturbance broke out during a performance by the British rock-and-roll musical group the Rolling Stones. Eleven youngsters were held in temporary custody in a detention room at the Pacific National Exhibition Forum during the show. Two were charged with being drunk. Police said a policeman was kicked in the groin, an usher suffered a concussion when hit by a youth, a policewoman collapsed from exhaustion and a youth suffered a broken ankle during the show. Officers said a number of hysterical girls had to be carried over a riot fence between the audience and the performers."

Fellow Englishmen the Who—guitarist Pete Townshend, singer Roger Daltrey, bassist John Entwistle and drummer Keith Moon—assailed the PNE Agrodome with their inherently violent and demonstrative stage show at

Singer Roger Daltrey and The Who first assailed Vancouver with their inherently violent and demonstrative show in 1967. Dee Lippingwell

Opposite: The Who's volatile guitarist Pete Townshend smashed his instrument during the Vancouver performance, only to discover it was the last one he had.
Dee Lippingwell

the height of 1967's "Summer of Love." Before the gig, the ever-entertaining Moon purchased a piranha, deposited it in his hotel room's bathtub and amused his roommate Entwistle by trying to "tickle its nose." When they returned to find Moon's pet dead in the cold bathwater, they gracefully proceeded to wrap it in a tissue to leave on the toilet seat as "a present" for the maid.

Guitarist/songsmith Townshend, meanwhile, well-known for smashing his instrument when the mood struck, did so as usual that night in Vancouver, only to discover it was the last one he had. A new guitar had to be purchased before the band could take the stage at their next stop in Salt Lake City, Utah. Following Moon's untimely (albeit none-too-surprising) demise on September 7, 1978, the surviving trio returned to Vancouver on several occasions with additional musicians (including ex-Faces' drummer Kenney Jones and journeyman keyboardist John "Rabbit" Bundrick), mounting mostly "farewell" or "reunion" tours. Notable among them was the band's blistering performance at the Pacific Coliseum, April 14, 1980. Following the show, band members turned up at Rohan's Rockpile on West Fourth Avenue and jammed. The previous evening, Townshend and entourage had shown up at the Commodore Ballroom around closing time and cajoled the staff into keeping the bar open and letting them drink.

The Shows You Don't Remember

"Those are the shows you remember," says Bruce Allen. "The Beatles at Empire Stadium, the Stones at the Forum—those were great shows. But what about the ones everybody forgets about? The Retinal Circus had Janis Joplin with Big Brother and the Holding Company, the Doors, Jimi Hendrix. Tommy Chong, later of Cheech and Chong fame, played guitar in bands like Four Niggers and a Chink, which became Bobby Taylor and the Vancouvers and had a big hit on Motown Records with 'Does Your Mama Know About Me?'"

One of the earliest (and briefest) of the Vancouvers was a then-unknown Seattle-born guitarist named Jimi Hendrix (a.k.a. Jimmy James), who was fired, according to Taylor in a 1998 interview, because "his solos went on too long, like about a half an hour, and he played his guitar so loud you couldn't hear the rest of the band." Living

Bobby Taylor and the Vancouvers were the first Canadian group signed to Motown Records. In turn, they later discovered the Jackson Five for Motown. Rob Frith Collection

BOBBY TAYLOR & THE VANCOUVERS

with his grandmother Nora at 827 East Georgia after being discharged from the US Army due to a parachute injury, Hendrix had a short but ear-splitting incarnation as a Vancouver R&B sideman. "He was just too goddamn loud. The waitress couldn't hear drink orders," affirmed Lachman Jir, owner of the Smilin' Buddha Cabaret on East Hastings.

Long before Jir's establishment became synonymous with punk rock and earned a reputation alongside New York's CBGB and London's 100 Club as an international hub for the genre, it catered to soul bands. Jir, who ran the dive for decades with his wife Nancy, laid claim to kicking Hendrix off the stage in the early 1960s when the guitarist refused to turn down his volume. "After the first set, Lachman laid down the law," says Vancouver musician and author John Armstrong (a.k.a. Modernettes' singer/guitarist Buck Cherry), who heard the story firsthand from Jir 20 years later, during punk's heyday. "Either the guitarist turned down or they could pack their shit up and leave. We made him tell us that story every few weeks. He couldn't understand the interest we had in this ancient event. 'Why do you care?' he'd say. 'Better guitar players here every night. You play better than him. I sell more drinks when you play.'"

But compared to another temporary stateside import, Hendrix hardly qualified as a fraud. "I remember a show at a place called Dante's Inferno on Davie Street," Allen recalls. "Eddie Floyd, who'd had a big hit with 'Knock on Wood,' was supposed to perform but Eddie Floyd never showed up. So the promoter drove down to Tacoma, Washington, and got a black guy who could sing, a garbage truck driver. We didn't know the

Above: The Smilin' Buddha Cabaret on East Hastings catered to soul bands before becoming home base for Vancouver's punk scene.
Ian Lindsay *Vancouver Sun*

Left: Jerry Lee Lewis had built up a storied history in Vancouver prior to returning for Red Robinson's "Legends of Rock 'n' Roll" program at Expo 86.
Red Robinson Collection

Texan Buddy Knox, a true rock and roll pioneer who began recording before Elvis Presley or Buddy Holly, moved to Vancouver in the early 1970s and opened the Purple Steer nightclub. Les Vogt Collection

difference. I'll never forget. This guy came out and did 'Knock on Wood' for 33 minutes because he didn't know any other songs, except maybe 'Soul Man' or something like that. The show had three songs and it went for an hour."

By the mid-1960s, major artists of the 1950s—generally given short shrift by unscrupulous managers and record companies during the peak years of their careers—began hitting the road out of financial desperation. Early rock and roller Jerry Lee Lewis ("the Killer") had enjoyed smash hits in the late 1950s with "Whole Lotta Shakin' Going On," "Great Balls of Fire" and "Breathless." In 1957, however, his career took a substantial pounding when he married his 13-year-old third cousin (and third wife) Myra Gale Brown. Although he wouldn't have another hit until switching to country music in the late sixties, he toured relentlessly. "When Jerry Lee Lewis came to town," says Allen, "he had a bodyguard with him whose only job was to follow Jerry Lee around the club after the show. Jerry Lee would get drunk and come out and try to hustle some guy's girlfriend. The guy would tell him to fuck off, Jerry Lee would snarl, 'What did you say?' and the bodyguard would step in and pound the shit out of the guy. It was ridiculous. But, of course, Jerry Lee Lewis didn't fight anybody because he'd get killed.

"Lewis's contract called for a suite with a piano in it, so they put him up in the Georgian Towers, and he would always have these parties afterwards up in his hotel suite," Allen continues. "We'd go up and he'd have his piano and be playing all these songs and then the broads would show up. One night, Jerry Lee got high on coke and decided he was going to throw empty champagne bottles out of his hotel window and try to hit the cars on Georgia Street. So he starts firing these fucking champagne bottles down at the cars and they're smashing all over Georgia Street and everywhere. Finally the cops came up and shut it down. Another time, he was coming to town and the promoter couldn't get him through Customs. Jerry Lee had flown up on this beaten-up 727 he was renting—it was a wonder it didn't crash—and he had 46 guns on it. The guy was unbelievable: a completely crazy bastard."

Pianist, singer and songwriter Charlie Rich—also known as "the Silver Fox," owing to his mane of thick grey hair—was markedly more sane. Although he'd placed "Lonely Weekends" in the Top 40 in 1960, huge crossover success eluded him until his singles "Behind Closed Doors" and "The Most Beautiful Girl" topped the charts in 1973. Rich was, therefore, all but ignored when he arrived in Vancouver in the late sixties to play the Purple Steer, a nightclub at Seymour and Davie owned by Les Vogt, Gary Taylor and Buddy Knox (the Texan singer who'd had a huge hit in 1957 with "Party Doll"). "Les Vogt and I booked him into the old Purple Steer but we couldn't get him any press," says Robinson. "Nobody wanted to interview him. A few years later, he came back to play a sold-out Coliseum in front of 16,000 people. So there we are backstage at the Coliseum before the show and there's a knock at the door. Somebody says, 'Mr. Rich the media is here waiting. You haven't talked to anyone from the media, yet.' Charlie Rich said, 'Tell 'em all to fuck off. I'm here with my friends who have always had time for me. Where were those people when I played the Purple Steer? Not one of those bastards would come and talk to me.'"

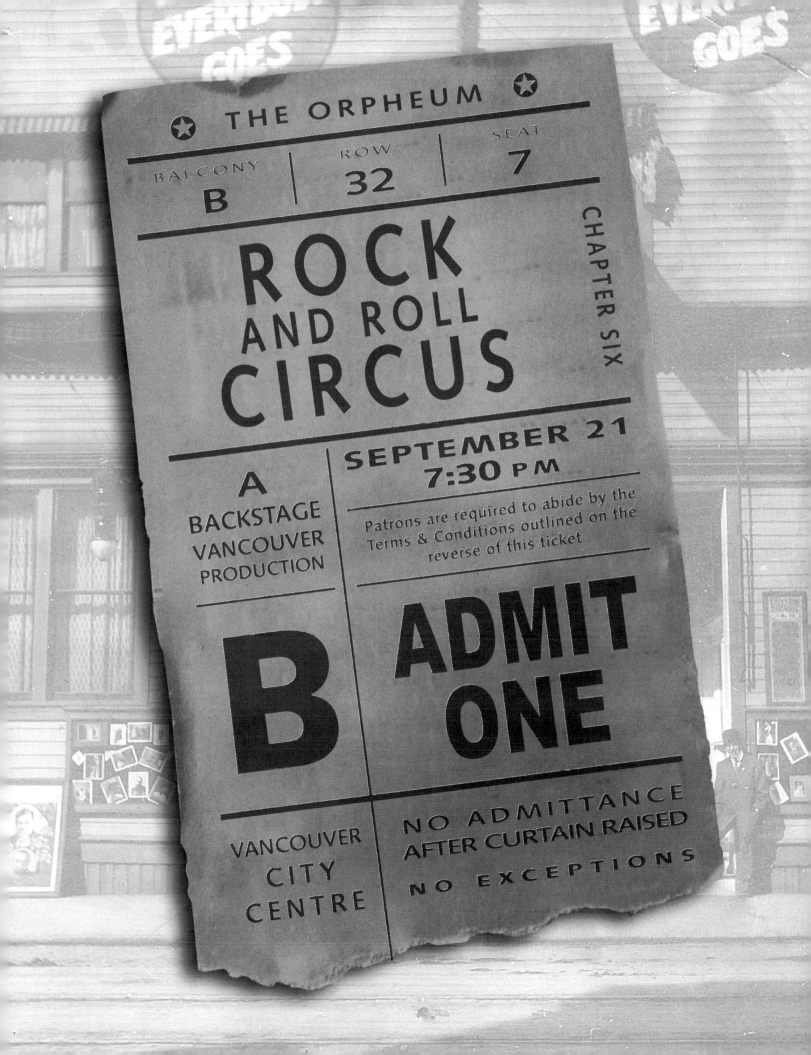

BACKSTAGE VANCOUVER

Jack Wasserman bemoaned the plight of the city's waning club scene in his *Vancouver Sun* column, January 13, 1970: "The problem is that many of the 'name' acts normally seen in a nightclub prefer to accept a one-night stand in the Queen Elizabeth Theatre or the Coliseum, where they can grab as big a fee for one night as they might otherwise receive for a week's work. For my part, I must confess a twinge of regret that the nightclub era is in temporary decline. If it comes to a choice, I think I'd rather see many entertainers in the smoky, slightly garish intimacy of a nightclub than in the austere confines of a large theatre or coliseum. Without nightclubs, Vancouver audiences will miss the opportunity to see the young performers on their way up. Then we can stay home and watch television." The truth of Wasserman's words rings loud and clear, in retrospect.

Some bands, however, didn't take a lot of time to find their way up to the stadium circuit. On August 19, 1971, the mighty British hard-rock quartet Led Zeppelin—singer Robert Plant, guitarist Jimmy Page, bassist/keyboardist John Paul Jones and drummer John Bonham—arrived at the Pacific Coliseum on the eve of Plant's 23rd birthday. An estimated 3,000 fans made the trek from Seattle and refused to be turned away. The crowd pushed on the arena's glass doors until promoters finally relented and let them in. The audience instantly swelled from 15,000 to 18,000 and the show had to be stopped twice in order for stagehands to push back the band's equipment because the front of the stage was torn apart by those grappling for space. To make matters worse, the band's gargantuan manager, Peter Grant, yanked a microphone-wielding man out of the rabble, dragged him backstage, beat him up, destroyed his equipment and threw him down a staircase, assuming that he was recording a bootleg of the concert. Grant later discovered that the unfortunate sod was a city ordinance official measuring the volume of the show.

Chaos continued to accompany rock shows in the early seventies, including performances by Rod Stewart and the Faces, the Rolling Stones and a revival revue featuring Chuck Berry, Jerry Lee Lewis, Bo Diddley and Bill Haley. A performance at the Agrodome by Frank Zappa and the Mothers of Invention was accompanied by

Left: Rod "The Mod" Stewart appeared with The Faces in Vancouver three times from 1970 through 1971. Dee Lippingwell

Opposite: Robert Plant of the mighty British hard-rock quartet Led Zeppelin had to cancel the band's 1973 encore after consuming a "spiked drink" backstage. Dee Lippingwell

BACKSTAGE VANCOUVER

One of the men responsible for starting it all, Chuck Berry, returned to Vancouver in the early seventies as part of a rock revival with Bo Diddley, Jerry Lee Lewis and Bill Haley. Craig Hodge

something else: cow manure. The Agrodome was a livestock showplace by day and, somehow, a quantity of the cattle industry's by-product got left behind during the change of shows. If Zappa noticed, he didn't object; perhaps he thought it a normal feature of Vancouver cultural outings.

Pop journalist Les Wiseman remembers running into Zappa in 1979 at Bud's Good Eats on Pacific, where he'd gone for a leisurely feed of ribs—so he thought.

"So here he is in Vancouver, salivating with this plate of delicious barbecued ribs in front of him," Wiseman recalls, "but every time he picks up his fork, some other media yobbo sits down across from him and says, 'Gee, Mr. Zappa, how come you're so weird?'" Apparently, the Polygram Records rep had set up interviews months in

Alice Cooper at the Pacific Coliseum in 1975. After tumbling from the stage, Cooper played one more song with his head bandaged. Craig Hodge

New York rock poet Lou Reed, here playing the Queen Elizabeth Theatre in 1976, went into ecstasies about Vancouver's scenic charms. Dee Lippingwell

advance and hadn't bothered warning him. Finally, Zappa just threw his napkin onto the plate and stormed off to the washroom. "I ran into him in there," Wiseman remembers, "and he looked at me and said, 'These fucking people. Why don't they just leave me the fuck alone.'" Zappa's disdain for the media was legendary.

One-time Zappa protegé Alice Cooper was a major star who had recently embarked on a solo career when he arrived at the Pacific Coliseum, June 23, 1975, with his highly theatrical *Welcome to My Nightmare* extravaganza. But early in the set, before a sold-out audience, the mascara-smeared shock rocker fell off the stage. "Even though he was always drinking in those days, he didn't seem pissed," says Wiseman. "Then again, he was a guy who could hold his liquor and never seemed to be drunk. He told me once when I interviewed him that he had a strict rule: he drank Budweiser beer all day but wouldn't touch his Canadian Club and Coke until 11 o'clock at night. Then he would get drunk. Whatever the case, he suddenly tumbled offstage, the lights came up and everybody said, 'What the fuck?' We all thought it was part of the act. He came out again and tried to do another song but his crew finally dragged him off and took him to the hospital." Cooper, who suffered six broken ribs in the incident (and stopped drinking in 1982) would later quip to reporters that his biggest disappointment was having to cancel a golf game the following day with his warm-up act, Suzi Quatro.

The following year, singer-songwriter Lou Reed brought his *Rock and Roll Heart* tour to the Queen Elizabeth Theatre and Wiseman interviewed him at the Holiday Inn Harbourside. "He was there with his inamorato at the time, the famous Rachel. Rachel was a Native-American transvestite, who was quite beautiful, with fine features and long shag hair. Lou was wearing this wretched denim leisure suit with flared trousers and the seams cut off so they were ragged at the end. I brought him a bottle of Johnny Walker Black because I'd heard he liked Scotch. But

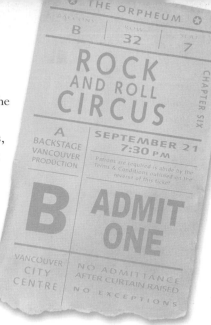

he had these dark prescription sunglasses on and he couldn't tell what it was. 'What the hell is this?' he kept saying, fumbling it around."

Despite just having gotten up and being well into his daily quota of Bloody Marys, Reed was getting full value from the sparkling view from the Harbourside's window. "Lou was just blown away by Coal Harbour. He was sitting there saying, 'Man, this is just like when Christopher Columbus arrived.'"

Raw Power

In 1974, Iggy Pop and the Stooges put in an appearance, of sorts, at the Pender Ballroom at 337 West Pender. Although the facility was licensed to hold 350 people, many more claim to have been crammed in the doors, including Art Bergmann and future Payola$ members Paul Hyde and Bob Rock.

"A lot of people consider that show to be a pivotal moment in Vancouver history," says Les Wiseman. "It was the catalyst that sparked the move from mainstream to alternative music. Only the cognoscenti knew who Iggy Pop was and what was amazing was that there was a whole sub-generation at that concert, none of whom knew each other at the time but all of whom would contribute in some way to what became Vancouver's alternative music and arts scenes. Everybody got there at 7 p.m. and many were taking chemicals. It was really hot and sweaty and people were peeling off their shirts. It was such a mind-bending experience, none of us were ever quite the same."

The Danny Tripper Band, the evening's warm-up act, ended up having to hit the stage three times from 8 to 11:30 p.m., with no sign of Iggy. Wiseman learned later that "Iggy had said to the promoters backstage, 'Where's the gratis drugs?' And they said, 'What gratis drugs?' Iggy said, 'If you expect me to go onstage, I need some blow or Preludins or MDA or Benzedrine or *something*. What do ya got?' So they had to send somebody down to Skid Row to procure some drugs. Well, whatever they got him, they sure got him some good stuff, because when he came out around midnight, he was just subhuman."

Clad in silver hot pants stretched over green nylons with calf-high black leather boots, no shirt and chrome-dyed hair, Iggy "stomped out of the wings like an ape," says Wiseman. "He grabbed the microphone and immediately started berating the crowd. Then James Williamson came out with jet-black Mr. Spock hair, red eyeshadow up to his eyebrows, pointy black sideburns and this open-chested black batwing outfit covered in sequins. He was teetering around on knee-high leather boots with huge stiletto heels. Suddenly, an ungodly screech of feedback assailed the crowd and the concert was on.

"Early in the show," Wiseman continues, "Iggy, who is about five-foot-nothing and 90 pounds, decided to start picking fights with people. He unscrewed his microphone stand, took out the centre part and started whacking audience members over the head with this hunk of metal. People were saying, 'Well, this is good. I came here to get killed and I waited five hours for it.' Lord knows what the people ripped on acid — and there were a lot of them there—were making of this chrome-haired goofball swinging a steel pipe at their skulls. It was a helluva show. Sheer unadulterated violence and aggression. It lasted maybe an hour. The crowning moment was when James Williamson thrashed his guitar until every string broke, at which point he threw it down and staggered off. That was the end of the show."

When Wiseman met Pop (real name: James Newell Osterberg) 13 years later, Iggy was wielding a different kind of metal: a Canadian platinum album for his 1986 release *Blah, Blah, Blah*. "He was clean and sober by then, wearing glasses, a sports coat and short hair," says Wiseman. "He was quite a gregarious and happy fellow, completely different from the way he was at the Pender Ballroom. After the presentation, we were walking through the Hotel Vancouver on the way to the photo shoot and I asked him how he kept in such good shape. He just looked at me and said, 'A lotta sex, man, a lotta sex.'"

Opposite: Iggy Pop's "subhuman" performance with the Stooges at the Pender Ballroom in 1974 inspired Vancouver's nascent punk scene. Dee Lippingwell

By the summer of 1977, the Stooges' sound had morphed into punk rock and a Burnaby lad named Joe Keithley christened himself "Joey Shithead" and begat D.O.A., one of the first and certainly the most resilient punk rock bands Canada ever produced. Meanwhile, Keithley's high school chums—Brian "Wimpy Roy" Goble, Gerry "Useless" Hannah and Ken "Dimwit" Montgomery—founded the Subhumans. The two groups provided the backbone for a scene that revolved around the Smilin' Buddha Cabaret on East Hastings (though any venue would suffice, including the Windmill on Granville, the Laundromat on Richards and whatever legion or cultural hall was available for rent).

Around this time, Dublin-born mouthpiece and everyman Bob Geldof worked for a spell as a *Georgia Straight* writer before returning to Ireland and forming the Boomtown Rats, which charted a minor North American hit in 1980 with "I Don't Like Mondays." In 1982, he starred in the film version of Pink Floyd's *The Wall* and, in 1985, organized the Live Aid concerts at London, England's Wembley Stadium and Philadelphia, Pennsylvania's JFK Stadium to raise funds for Ethiopian famine victims. His humanitarian efforts garnered him an honourary knighthood and a Nobel Peace Prize nomination the following year.

Keithley doesn't recall Geldof being so chivalrous in his Vancouver days. "Bob Geldof once called me a 'fucking

Vancouver's pre-eminent punk band D.O.A. in their habitat, with (l-r) Joe "Shithead" Keithley, Brian "Wimpy Roy" Goble (seated), Chris Prohom and Jon Card.
Steve Bosch
Vancouver Sun

ROCK
AND ROLL
CIRCUS

A
BACKSTAGE
VANCOUVER
PRODUCTION

SEPTEMBER 21
7:30 PM

Patrons are required to abide by the
terms & Conditions outlined on the
reverse of this ticket

B ADMIT
ONE

VANCOUVER
CITY
CENTRE

NO ADMITTANCE
AFTER CURTAIN RAISED

NO EXCEPTIONS

idiot' on the back steps of the *Georgia Straight* offices," says Keithley. "Somebody introduced us, and as I was walking away, I heard him say, 'Ah, that fuckin' idiot.' I never had anything against him prior to that, and it's good that he organized those benefits, but they far surpassed his musical abilities."

By the early 1980s, groups from up and down the West Coast—X, Black Flag, the Minutemen and the Circle Jerks from Los Angeles; the Dead Kennedys, the Nuns and the Dils from San Francisco—shared bills and tours with D.O.A. and the Subhumans, as well as other frontline Vancouver bands, including the Pointed Sticks, the Young Canadians, the Modernettes and 54-40. The communal training ground yielded a remarkable array of talents destined to establish themselves in various disciplines, among them musician/actor/activist Keithley, singer-songwriter Art Bergmann, singer/actor John Doe, singer/poet Exene Cervenka, poet/vocalist/actor Henry Rollins, vocalist/actor/activist Jello Biafra and singer-songwriter Alejandro Escovedo. With Keithley steadfast at the helm, D.O.A. celebrated its 25th anniversary in 2003 with the release of a remastered compilation album, *War and Peace*, in addition to Keithley's autobiography *I, Shithead.*

"People had a perception of punk rock as being nihilistic," says Keithley, "or else they didn't understand it at all. We were just a bunch of middle-class kids from the suburbs who knew that the rock and roll that was popular at the time absolutely stank. Locally, Prism topped the list as the worst band of all time and I always make sure to

Bob Geldof playing with the Boomtown Rats, 1980. Geldof's career as a small-time Vancouver journalist ended when he was deported, setting him on the path to world fame.
Dee Lippingwell

Above: British punk rock trail-blazers The Clash (above, left to right: Joe Strummer, Mick Jones and Paul Simonon) clashed with hometown punk band D.O.A. in 1979. Dee Lippingwell

Left: Punker Joe "Shithead" Keithley of D.O.A., the self-styled "big crazy lumberjack" who intimidated fretful members of The Clash, liked to rev up his chainsaw on stage, once accidentally bloodying a finger. Here he plays in the tamer surroundings of a peace rally. Stuart Davis *Vancouver Sun*

thank them for inspiring me to get into punk rock. The Eagles were right up there, too. What a bunch of bullshit. It was the apex of that really bad rock era, circa 1976 to '77. Coupled with disco, those were the only two flavours on the menu. Then I heard the Ramones in 1976 and immediately thought, 'Okay, something's happening here.' You can't have rock music without rebellion; otherwise, it becomes way too businesslike."

Keithley discovered, firsthand, just how phony the rock industry could be when his band opened for British punk rock trailblazers the Clash—guitarists/vocalists Joe Strummer and Mick Jones, bassist Paul Simonon and drummer Topper Headon—at the PNE Forum on October 16, 1979, during the band's *Give 'Em Enough Rope* tour. Vancouver punk fans had fond memories of the foursome playing the Commodore Ballroom the previous year. Band members had even challenged members of the local media to a good-natured soccer match. Things were a bit more formal this time around.

"We held the Clash in high ideal," says Keithley. "We put them up on a pedestal. But when we were asked to open for them, we ended up waiting around for hours for a sound check that never happened. Somebody had a little kid there, who was maybe four or five years old, and Mick Jones—who was always the wanker of the band, if you ask me—started trying to teach this kid how to play drums when we were supposed to be doing our sound check. And it wasn't just us who missed a sound check. The Rockabilly Rebels, who were the other warm-up band, missed theirs, too, because Jones was too busy farting around with this kid. So we were a little sour about that. Then we got our set cut short and we were pretty fucking pissed off. Everybody thought the Clash was a 'friend-of-the-people' kinda band because of their political stance but they weren't really that kind of a band at all. They were a premeditated band, the same as the Sex Pistols. Their manager was pretty sharp and he picked the right cast and crew. That doesn't take away from the fact that they wrote great songs but they just weren't what they appeared to be.

"The thing that really amazed me," Keithley continues, "was how short all of these guys were. Just little tiny guys. So I blocked their entrance to the stage when it was time for them to go on. As each one of them walked up, I yelled and screamed in his face, 'You guys are a lot of bullshit, y'know that?!' Joe Strummer, in particular, looked pretty scared, like 'Uh, oh, this crazy lumberjack is going to kill me.' Instead of that, we just went back to their dressing room and stole all their beer."

While the Clash was onstage, the antagonism escalated and spilled into the audience. "A bunch of people started catcalling Mick Jones," Keithley says. "They were yelling, 'Why'd you fuck around D.O.A.? When did you guys become such a bunch of rock stars?' Finally, a guy challenged Mick Jones to a fight and Jones went to the lip of the stage and started screaming, 'You come up here!' It was a real confrontation. Every time the lights went down between songs, Jones was bombarded with empty beer cans. After the show, our friend David Spaner saw Mick Jones and said to him, 'What happened? You guys had such a great time in Vancouver the last time you were here, but this time, it wasn't very cool.' Jones snapped, 'We'll never come back to this shit-hole town again and we hate that crappy heavy metal band that opened up for us. D.O.A. suck!' So a bunch of our fans went out and spray-painted their tour bus with graffiti: 'D.O.A. Rules—The Clash Suck!' I would have loved to have seen Mick Jones's face when he came out the next day and saw his bus."

You Gotta Choose Your Medicine

The 1980s plunked Vancouver on the world stage for all to see. Canada's first domed stadium, the 60,000-seat BC Place, opened in 1983, and the following year, the Jacksons—Michael, Tito, Randy, Jackie and Marlon—played a three-night stand at the colossal structure, grossing several million dollars and setting a Vancouver entertainment-attendance record. In 1984, Pope John Paul II paid the town its first papal visit, and the planet's populace was invited en masse to Expo 86. Twenty-two million showed up, eight million more than anticipated.

During Expo, another icon with a devout worldwide following descended on BC Place. On a gruelling summer-

Above: Roy Orbison was one of the superstars Red Robinson secured to play for Expo 86's "Legends of Rock 'n' Roll" program. Others included Ray Charles, Fats Domino, Jerry Lee Lewis and the Righteous Brothers. Red Robinson Collection

Opposite: Bob Dylan also played Vancouver during Expo 86, afterwards gifting an impressive stock of unused booze to the delighted hotel bellman. Here, Dylan plays the Pacific Coliseum on Remembrance Day 1978. Dee Lippingwell

long tour, Bob Dylan stopped in Vancouver on August 1, 1986, settling in at Hornby Street's posh Wedgewood Hotel. "We always knew who was coming to the hotel in advance," says Don Prior, who was working his way through university as a bellman. "I wangled it so I was working the morning shift the day after the concert, when Dylan was checking out.

"I went up to his room," Prior continues, "and Dylan was wearing sunglasses and a black leather fringe coat and there were bottles of everything in his suite—Wild Turkey, all kinds of wine, you name it—and he was definitely wired but not in a booze-like way. He was walking around really fast and he was really jittery. On top of that, he had this hyperkinetic manager who was buzzing around all over, making sure everything was okay before they checked out. When his manager was leaving to round up the other band members, he said to me, 'You keep an eye on Bob.' It was like working at Inglewood Hospital during a full moon. I think his manager was afraid Dylan was going to escape or something. So I stayed with Bob for about half an hour or 45 minutes and just started talking to him. I mean, what else are you going to do, right?"

Meanwhile, Burl Ives, the rotund actor and folksinger (best known for playing Big Daddy opposite Paul Newman and Elizabeth Taylor in 1958's *Cat on a Hot Tin Roof* and narrating the Yuletide favourite *Rudolph the Red-*

Lead singer Kurt Cobain of the seminal grunge band Nirvana played two of the last shows of his final North American tour at Vancouver's PNE Forum in 1994. Three months later he shot himself at his Seattle home. Peter Battistoni *Vancouver Sun*

B | 32 | 7

ROCK
AND ROLL
CIRCUS

A
BACKSTAGE
VANCOUVER
PRODUCTION

SEPTEMBER 21
7:30 PM

Patrons are required to abide by the
terms & conditions outlined on the
reverse of this ticket

B ADMIT ONE

VANCOUVER
CITY
CENTRE

NO ADMITTANCE
AFTER CURTAIN RAISED
NO EXCEPTIONS

CHAPTER SIX

Nosed Reindeer) was staying in the suite directly below Dylan's. "Burl was staying at the Wedgewood for a month," says Prior, "and I'd gotten to know him pretty well. I knew he was a folksinger, so I said, 'I should hook you up with Bob Dylan. He's right upstairs.' Ives said, 'Oh, Bob Dylan. He's a great American.' Burl was right into it. British folksinger Billy Bragg was staying there that night, too, so I thought, 'Hmm, the father, the son and the holy ghost.' I thought it would be great to pull them all together. Maybe they could jam or something.

"But as soon as I mentioned it to Dylan," Prior continues, "he wanted absolutely nothing to do with it. He didn't want anything to do with Burl Ives. Dylan said, 'Oh, man, he named names!'" Ives had been blacklisted as a suspected communist in the early 1950s by US Senator Joseph McCarthy's House Un-American Activities Committee, along with Dylan's idols and mentors Woody Guthrie and Pete Seeger. Ives, however—unlike Guthrie and Seeger—had "named names" of other suspected communists, in order to save his own hide. As for Billy Bragg, "Dylan didn't know who he was," says Prior.

On his way out, Dylan seemed momentarily befuddled over how to tip Prior. "He's Bob Dylan, right?" says Prior. "He didn't have any cash or money on him. So he waved his hand, gesturing to all the booze in the room—there must have been about two dozen bottles—and he said, 'Hey, it's all yours.' So I ended up with this Wild Turkey that I doled out to my friends, in thimbles, for about a year. It was kind of like a shrine."

In the late eighties, another frequently deified, era-defining figure began to make appearances in Vancouver, though at that point, Kurt Cobain was merely a pint-sized punk rocker from the nearby logging community of Aberdeen, Washington. Proximity naturally dictated that the tsunami of early-nineties Seattle-area "grunge" bands—Nirvana, Soundgarden, Mudhoney, Pearl Jam, Tad, Alice in Chains, Screaming Trees, et al.—would invariably hit Vancouver, mostly at soon-to-be-defunct clubs such as the Town Pump on Gastown's Water Street.

Nirvana, and razor-throated vocalist/guitarist Kurt Cobain in particular, put on a stupendous stage show. Whether flinging himself into the drum kit, slamming into amplifier stacks or colliding with six-foot-seven-inch bassist Krist Novoselic, Cobain was a man on a mission to self-destruct. Three years, a highly publicized heroin habit and at least one suicide attempt later, the 27-year-old Cobain finally fulfilled his mission, by way of a self-inflicted shotgun wound on April 5, 1994. One of the most famous photographs taken over the course of his life was by Charles Peterson at the Commodore Ballroom on March 8, 1991. Cobain is captured in a rock-guitarist pose unrivalled by even Pete Townshend or Jimi Hendrix, playing a solo with his legs straight up in the air and the back of his neck planted on the stage. Over the next decade, several visiting performers made headlines with their own theatrics onstage—or, just as likely, offstage.

While opening for Lenny Kravitz at the Pacific Coliseum in October 1993, Blind Melon played three full songs with their singer Shannon Hoon wandering the stage stark naked. Hoon topped off his performance by urinating into the crowd. Vancouver police chose not to arrest him onstage for fear of inciting a riot but blocked the band's bus from leaving the arena after the concert. Hoon climbed out one of the bus's windows and onto its roof, unleashing a string of obscenities

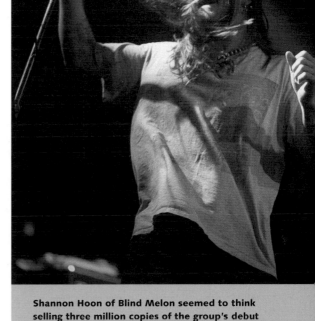

Shannon Hoon of Blind Melon seemed to think selling three million copies of the group's debut album gave him the right to urinate on Vancouver fans. He was wrong.
Peter Battistoni *Vancouver Sun*

Above: Singer Gordon Downie of the Canadian megastars Tragically Hip plays the tiny Railway Club in 1996. The group used to play the Railway in their days as an unknown bar band. Dee Lippingwell

Opposite: After being pelted with shoes at the Coliseum in 1996, Noel Gallagher and Oasis boldly returned to Vancouver for a GM Place gig in 1998. This time they put on a much better show and avoided the shoes. Dee Lippingwell

at the top of his lungs. After he was convinced to come down, the police incarcerated him and charged him with committing an indecent act and public nudity. "I don't know what he was high on," said Constable Jack Froese, "but we lodged him in jail for a while, as is our normal practice for people in this shape." Two years later, Hoon died of a drug overdose.

Conspicuously Absent

When Canadian troubadour Gordon Lightfoot stormed off the Queen Elizabeth Theatre stage mid-show in 1977 after admonishing some knucklehead for setting off firecrackers during his performance, he sent a shock wave through the concert-going community. Short of the Doors' Jim Morrison, who had his own reasons for either leaving or being dragged off concert stages on a regular basis, this type of behaviour was simply unheard of. Not so in the 1990s.

On February 2, 1995, a special evening at Vancouver's cozy, 200-seat Railway Club with two members of the monstrous British band Radiohead went awry when temperamental singer/guitarist Thom Yorke threw a hissy fit. "It was a little after-work media event that EMI, the band's record label, had arranged for the release of the band's second album, *The Bends*," says the Railway's co-owner and manager Janet Forsyth. "The place was packed and many Radiohead fans had come early, so they were well-oiled by the time Thom and guitarist Jonny Greenwood took the stage. There was a table of fans who kept screaming for them to play 'Creep,' the big hit off their first record, and Thom was getting increasingly pissed at them and mouthing off quite a bit. Finally, he just stormed off the stage after about the fourth song and wouldn't come back. Jonny, however, was really nice and stuck around and talked to people in the bar."

The notoriously pugnacious Gallagher brothers of Oasis fame—vocalist Liam and guitarist Noel—were considerably less cordial after the Manchester quintet was pelted with, among other things, coins and shoes during

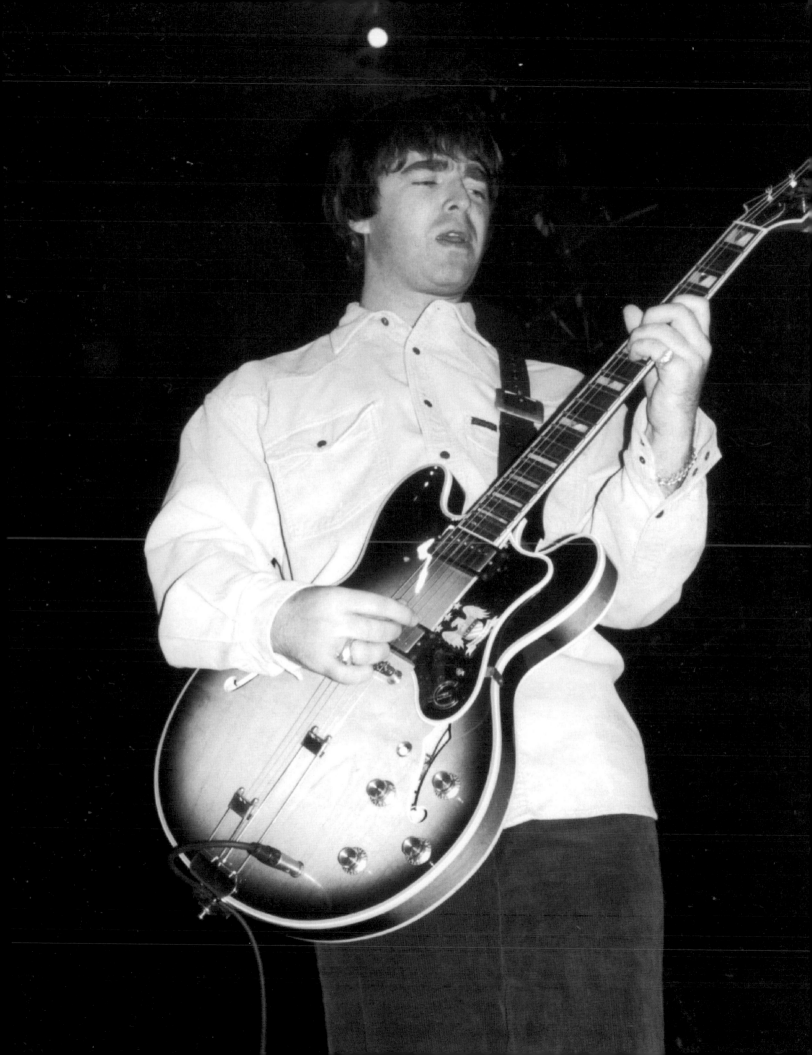

Phil Collins plays a solo concert at the Pacific Coliseum in 1990. Dee Lippingwell

a concert at the Pacific Coliseum, April 11, 1996. After several more projectiles including hats, soccer balls and still more shoes cascaded onto the stage, the band left, 20 minutes into the show. When the crowd began booing, Liam, smoke in hand, stormed back out and scolded the audience before making his final exit: "You shouldn't be throwing shoes at us. We're not a bunch of fucking monkeys. We're the best band in the world!"

When another narcissistic singer of note, Axl Rose, failed to even turn up on time for his Guns N' Roses concert at GM Place, November 7, 2002, promoters opted to pull the plug just prior to showtime. A riot broke out as thousands of unruly fans commenced to break windows, trash Ticketmaster kiosks and throw firecrackers at security, swiftly doing damage estimated in the several hundred-thousand-dollar range. Police arrived and retaliated with pepper spray and batons. The following day, Rose told a Seattle radio station that, despite missing sound check and being in a plane at the time the concert was cancelled, he had still planned to make it for the band's scheduled 9:30 p.m. start time. He added that he was considering legal action against GM Place.

They were different times, indeed, when on May 20, 1980, Phil Collins personally apologized to Genesis fans outside the Pacific Coliseum for having to cancel the evening's concert because he had strained his voice during sound check. Incidentally, Genesis released the single "Vancouver" in June 1978, an ode to Collins's failed marriage to Andrea Bertorelli, who relocated to the city in the late 1970s with the couple's children, Simon and Joely. The latter, who was adopted by Collins shortly after the marriage ended, went on to become a successful Vancouver-based television actor.

The same year Axl pulled his no-show, the similarly volatile Courtney Love did manage to arrive in Vancouver in 2002 and stayed for a month while filming *Trapped* with Charlize Theron and Kevin Bacon. Never one to shy away from headlines, one night the singer/songwriter/actor hopped onstage at Richard's on Richards alongside rocker Evan Dando and promptly flashed her breasts. Shortly thereafter, she waltzed out of a dressing room in Alberni Street fashion boutique Bruce completely naked, dragging her daughter behind her. After complaining that $10,000 worth of jewellery had been stolen from her Pacific Palisades hotel room, she announced that she'd also suffered a miscarriage during her stay. In parting, Kurt Cobain's widow declared that Vancouverites were "spineless pushovers" and slinked out of town without anteing up for a waterfront mansion she'd rented.

BACKSTAGE VANCOUVER

Despite Courtney Love's opinion of Vancouver residents, the city's history of hosting performers includes a long-standing reputation among major-league filmmakers and television producers as a viable alternative to Hollywood. Although movies had been shot in the Lower Mainland since the early 20th century—the dramatic short, *The Cowpuncher's Glove*, was filmed at North Van's Capilano Suspension Bridge in 1910—it wasn't until influential American director Robert Altman shot 1969's *That Cold Day in the Park* in town that the foundations were laid for what would become "Hollywood North."

Yet, despite ever-rising production budgets and an ever-plummeting Canadian dollar, Hollywood was unloading mostly B-grade throwaways on the city during the seventies: 1972's *The Groundstar Conspiracy* with George Peppard (later a recovering alcoholic, he was remembered by more than one crew member as "a drunken sonofabitch"), 1974's *Christina* starring Vancouver-born *Playboy* pin-up Barbara Parkins (previously featured in the sixties soap *Peyton Place* and 1967's *Valley of the Dolls* opposite Sharon Tate, who asked Parkins to be a bridesmaid at her 1968 wedding to director Roman Polanski) and 1975's *Russian Roulette* with George Segal (better known locally by its well-publicized working title, *Kosygin Is Coming*).

Sandy Dennis and Michael Burns in Robert Altman's *That Cold Day in the Park* (1969), arguably the first major American film to be shot in Vancouver.

Vancouver's dazzling Theatre Row in 1970.
Ralph Bower

American Cousins

"Any discussion of Vancouver as a film-production capital has to start with *McCabe and Mrs. Miller*," says Vancouver broadcaster, actor and television host Terry David Mulligan. Although it was no great shakes at the box office, Altman's 1970 "anti-hero western" was the biggest production undertaken in Vancouver up to that time and it helped put the town on the moviemaking map. Mulligan got on as an extra and remembers it as something of a bizarre experience.

In keeping with the spirit of the times, Altman not only constructed a Pacific Northwest-style frontier town, he had cast and crew members live on the set. "It was very organic, very hippie-driven," says Mulligan. "We were shooting in a sawmill up near Squamish that had been built around a small town. By some perverse luck, the buildings had been preserved and Altman constructed some of his own, as well."

Like a lot of Altman's films, this one was largely made up as they went along. Mulligan remembers one unexpectedly arduous day, in particular. "It was 8:30 or 9 o'clock in the morning and I'm in the barn with all the other extras, wearing a huge buffalo coat. It was very likely that we were not going to work that day, so we're smoking a joint to ward off the cold. Just as we finish, I hear over the two-way radio: 'Ask Terry Mulligan to come to the set.'"

Mulligan was summoned to appear in a pivotal scene at the bar in which John McCabe (Warren Beatty) arrives in town to pick up the hookers for a brothel he is opening with Mrs. Miller (Julie Christie). No sooner had they got him in position than Altman instructed the actor playing the bartender to 'Pour the boy a drink.' Altman had insisted that all the liquor be real—in this case, white lightning made by the bartender himself—and that Mulligan's glass be refilled after every re-take. "We started shooting at 10 o'clock in the morning and I'd had nothing to eat," Mulligan says. "By the time we wrapped at two o'clock in the afternoon, if Altman had given me a line to say, I simply couldn't have formed the words. I was a complete and total mess."

Another local on the set was Chinatown elder Harvey Lowe, who proved invaluable when Christie wanted to get into character as an opium smoker. Lowe used his Chinatown connections, and $100 cash, to entice an old-time smoker to the set. "She wants you to explain how they smoke opium," Lowe told the user. "She wants to smoke it like a real addict." The scene of Christie dissolving into an opium trance became one of the most memorable images in the film, though what it had to do with the story would be hard to say.

Altman, a committed improviser ever in pursuit of spontaneity, generally hated squandering time and money on multiple takes. Beatty was his polar opposite, a pragmatic perfectionist who badgered directors to distraction with his relentless nitpicking. But Altman got his own back.

In the film's closing sequence, Beatty's character falls dying into a snowdrift. "Warren was buried up to his ears, with snow blasting into his face from the wind machine," recalled production manager Jim Margellos in Peter Biskind's book *Easy Riders, Raging Bulls*. "It was colder than hell. Bob kept saying, 'Okay, one more time.' They dug Warren out, put him back and did it again. He must have done it 25 times." The sequence would become known among the film's inner circle as "Altman's revenge."

"Everybody liked Altman a lot and the crew busted a hump for him," says Mulligan. "He gave many Vancouver actors and crew members their first big breaks because he liked their attitude. It was a throwback to another time and place for him. There was no cynicism here and he loved that fact.

"That movie was originally called *Presbyterian Church Wager* and Altman gave out posters to the cast and crew with that title on them. They were beautifully done and looked like they'd been made back in the 1890s. I hung onto mine and gave it to Altman when I interviewed him in 2002, while he was in Vancouver shooting a pilot. He hadn't kept one for himself and he freaked when he saw it. He thanked me profusely and said, 'It all comes back to me. Man, there are a lot of memories there.'"

Director Mike Nichols turned up in town shortly after Altman to shoot 1971's *Carnal Knowledge*. With Vancouver standing in for New York City, the film chronicled the sexual mores of two pals, played by Jack Nicholson and Art Garfunkel, over a 30-year period. The movie also starred 24-year-old Candice Bergen, a model/photographer/actress desperately trying to escape the unhip stigma of being ventriloquist Edgar Bergen's daughter. (Her father's wooden dummy, Charlie McCarthy, occupied a bigger bedroom and owned a larger wardrobe than she did as a child.) Attending a function one evening during her stay, Bergen was accosted by *Sun* columnist Wasserman, finally losing her temper and screaming at him, "Will you just leave me alone?! I'm not going to give you an interview!" To which Wasserman shot back, "Oh, yeah? Well, your father moves his lips!"

Hollywood's Back Lot

According to the BC Film Commission, in 1978 the film and television industry spent $12 million in the province. By 2003, that number had swelled to $1.405 billion. Roughly 50,000 residents rely on the industry for their livelihood and more than 90 percent of the crew members working in the province are British Columbians. With 40 projects on the go at any one time, 169 productions were shot in 2003, including 69 foreign ones. Of the Canadian projects, 47 were feature films, 79 were for television and six were animation, which included *I Robot*, *Paycheck*, *Scary Movie 3*, *Scooby-Doo 2*, *Elf*, *Unfinished Life*, *Cat Woman*, *Chronicles*

Filming of *The 4400*, USA Network's popular cable-TV series shot in Vancouver. Copyright 2004 Alan Zenuk Universal Television Networks

When Vancouver starlet Dorothy Stratten appeared on *The Tonight Show* in 1980, flustered host Johnny Carson blurted, "You are as beautiful in person as you are in your photos!"
Wayne Leidenfrost *The Province*

of Riddick, Miracle on Ice, MuchMusic Movie, White Noise, Pursued, Smallville, Stargate, Deadzone, DaVinci's Inquest, The Collector and *Andromeda*. Vancouver ranks as the third largest film production centre in North America, after Los Angeles and New York. It's small wonder Chris Carter, *The X-Files'* creator, writer and producer, dubbed the city "Hollywood's biggest back lot."

"I remember, during the seventies, that there were so few jobs we were all fighting over one or two bit parts a year," says Terry David Mulligan. "It was a big deal to have a feature film shot in Vancouver because there was very little work going on. When people got work, they really appreciated it." Mulligan relocated to San Francisco in 1980 and returned in 1983 to find dramatic changes had taken place. "All of a sudden, the industry really started to roll and everybody was elated but they kept thinking, 'Well, the bottom is going to drop out, so let's enjoy it while we can.' But the bottom didn't drop out. It just kept getting bigger and bigger because of the greed, attitude and cynicism in Los Angeles. Hollywood just kept upping the price, thinking the industry had nowhere else to go. But once the producers and studios discovered an alternative, you couldn't keep them out. The whole idea that we stole

Clint Eastwood, Bryan Adams and Bruce Allen on location at the set of the Eastwood movie *Pink Cadillac*. Bruce Allen Collection

their business is absolute hogwash. Hollywood drove the business to us by thinking they were the only game in town."

Vancouver-born director Daryl Duke, whose credits include the 1973 film version of Margaret Craven's novel *I Heard the Owl Call My Name* as well as 1976's *Shadow of the Hawk*, both set in West Coast Native communities, was given the nod to direct the 1983 TV miniseries *The Thorn Birds* and the 1986 feature film *Tai-Pan*. Vancouver director Sandy Wilson, meanwhile, unleashed 1985's surprise hit, *My American Cousin*, and its follow-up, 1989's *American Boyfriends*, homegrown semi-autobiographical films starring Canadian-born actress Margaret Langrick.

Hollywood North got its biggest boost, however, courtesy of well-funded American productions such as 1982's *First Blood* (part one in Sylvester Stallone's *Rambo* series), 1983's *Star 80* (director Bob Fosse's lurid biopic of Vancouver-born *Playboy* Playmate Dorothy Stratten), 1984's *The NeverEnding Story* (and locally shot sequels which would follow in 1989 and 1996), 1988's *The Accused* (for which Jodie Foster won a Best Actress Oscar) and, in 1989 alone, *Look Who's Talking* (with John Travolta and Kirstie Alley), *We're No Angels* (with Robert De Niro, Sean Penn and Demi Moore), *Who's Harry Crumb?* (with John Candy) and *Bird on a Wire* (with Mel Gibson and Goldie Hawn).

TV Eye

Long before *Wiseguy*, *21 Jump Street*, *MacGyver*, *Neon Rider* and *The X-Files* set up shop in Vancouver, the city—or more accurately the nearby, water-access community of Gibsons on the Sunshine Coast—was home base for CBC's *The Beachcombers*. The show occupied a weekly spot on an average 1.5 million Canadian TV sets from 1972 to 1989 and revolved around the comedic exploits of West Coast lumber salvager Nick Adonidas (Bruno Gerussi), his pesky nemesis Relic (Robert Clothier), local cop Constable John Constable (Jackson Davies) and café-owner Molly (Rae Brown), who ran the landmark diner Molly's Reach.

The Beachcombers, an unlikely Vancouver-produced drama about a Greek guy and an Indian (Bruno Gerussi and Pat John) looking for logs, enjoyed an incredible 19-year run on CBC television. Roy Luckow

BACKSTAGE VANCOUVER

One of the longest-running, most popular and most widely syndicated Canadian TV shows ever, reaching 31 countries in five languages, the series provided a training ground for regional producers, directors, cinematographers, writers and actors, including Helen Shaver (*The Color of Money*), Bruce Greenwood (*Thirteen Days*) and Ryan Stiles (*The Drew Carey Show*). Its recurring cast, meanwhile, featured classically trained Canuck-born actors, including Shakespearean Stratford Festival star Gerussi.

"Bruno started in stage, playing Romeo at Stratford in the 1950s," says Bill Millerd, artistic managing director of Vancouver's Arts Club Theatre Company since 1972. "He was a real prankster and I remember, in particular, a play he did for us in 1994 called *Breaking Legs*, one year before he died. It was about a Mafia-type family and took place in an Italian restaurant with Bruno playing a kind of *Godfather*-like part, though all in good fun—pre-*Sopranos*. We were doing a fundraiser during the run and one of the things we auctioned off was a walk-on part in the play. The gentleman who won turned out to be a lawyer. All he had to do was come into the restaurant setting and order a meal; he didn't have any lines. But once the poor guy got onstage, Bruno started improvising and wouldn't let him leave. He kept him on the spot for ages, prodding him on and basically embarrassing the man, though, of course, it was all in good fun. We found out later that this fellow had bought 100 tickets and given them to his friends to see him onstage, so it all turned out rather well, despite the fact that he hadn't intended becoming such an integral part of the evening's performance."

Hollywood superstar Michael J. Fox made his professional stage debut at the Arts Club in the fall of 1978, though the Edmonton-born actor (who had relocated with his family to Burnaby in 1971 at age 10) had starred in the short-lived CBC-TV sitcom *Leo and Me* two years earlier. "Michael was in a show called *The Shadow Box*," says Millerd. "In those days, the cast members, of which there were nine, all shared one dressing room in a very little theatre we had at the corner of Seymour and Davie Streets. Being a teenager, he was full of vim and vigour, always incredibly enthusiastic and running around like a caged animal, bouncing off the walls. Of course, the older veteran actors were constantly trying to get him to calm down but Michael used that energy to propel himself onstage. Indeed, he was playing a kid in the show, and with his first entrance, he literally ran onto the stage.

Michael takes a breather between holes at a fundraising golf tournament for the Michael J. Fox Theatre, June 2003.
Gerry Kahrmann *Vancouver Sun*

Opposite: Michael J. Fox playing with the Vancouver Symphony Orchestra at the Orpheum Theatre in 1987. Dee Lippingwell

"Soon after the show had finished its run," Millerd continues, "Michael turned up outside the theatre, in the parking lot, in a truck. He was 18 at the time and said he was on his way to LA. I asked him, 'Why are you going to LA?' He said, 'I want to break into movies.' Now, obviously, people say that all the time. But I remember remarking to someone as he drove off, 'Well, he certainly has the drive.' You could just tell, right away, that if anybody was going to make it, he had the determination and the optimism and he wasn't going to be daunted."

Although Fox admittedly lived off Kraft Dinner during his first few years in Hollywood, he eventually scored starring roles in television's *Family Ties* (1982 to 1989), as well as the 1985 box-office smash *Back to the Future* (reprising his Marty McFly character in 1989 and 1990 sequels). After two years as creator, executive producer and lead actor in the popular TV series *Spin City*, Fox revealed, in 1998, that he had been diagnosed with Parkinson's disease, a degenerative disorder affecting the central nervous system. In January 2000, he announced that he was leaving the show (though he subsequently returned for a handful of cameos). In a bizarre coda, a March 2002 news story reported that three more members of the *Leo and Me* crew had been diagnosed with Parkinson's, citing environmental toxins or a virus linked to influenza as possible causes. An expert from the Pacific Parkinson's Research Centre commented, "This is one in 20,000. It's not a coincidence."

Blame It On the Rain

In 1993, actor David Duchovny went in the opposite direction by leaving LA for Vancouver, to star in the sci-fi TV series *The X-Files* as FBI Special Agent Fox Mulder. The move made him an international star, but four years later, he'd had enough … rain. "Vancouver is a very nice place if you like 400 inches of rainfall a day," Duchovny told *Late Night* host Conan O'Brien. "It is kind of like a tropical rainforest without the tropics. More like an Ice Age rainforest."

But in 2004, after returning to the city to act in Nia Varalos's *Connie and Carla*, Duchovny expressed some dramatic regret over the comments he'd made a decade earlier (perhaps to save his hide): "I'm starting to look

for land up there to buy because I apologized all I could and it seems the only thing I can do is actually move up there to prove that I love it, which I do. So I will stop at nothing to actually show that I love Vancouver. I will move there if I have to and live the rest of my life in Vancouver. It's a beautiful city."

Detroit-born actor Michael Moriarty appears to agree, despite his various tribulations. Appearing opposite Robert De Niro in 1973's *Bang the Drum Slowly* and Clint Eastwood in 1985's *Pale Rider*, Moriarty was probably best known for playing assistant district attorney Ben Stone from 1990 to 1994 in TV's long-running *Law & Order* series—that is, until he moved to Canada in 1996. A self-described "functioning alcoholic," he initially landed in Halifax but journeyed west to Vancouver after sidestepping charges arising from a bar-room brawl. Once he arrived, he picked up where he left off in November 2000, getting arrested for assault after slapping girlfriend/manager Margaret Brychka at Milestone's restaurant on Robson Street. Moriarty turned up next at the Wolf Pub in Maple Ridge, where five men gave him a "broken nose, damaged eye and wrecked shoulder." He described the attack as "the price of fame. Because I'm a high-profile, blatant drinker and smoker, I'm an easy target." It was soon revealed that Moriarty had been involved in three

Detroit-born film actor Michael Moriarty played opposite Robert de Niro and Clint Eastwood before moving to Vancouver. He is best known for his role as district attorney Ben Stone in the original *Law and Order*. Sam Feldman

X-Files star David Duchovny, infamous for accusing Vancouver of having an "ice-age" climate, enjoys a 1998 Grizzlies basketball game with his wife, Tea Leoni. Colin Price *The Province*

Wyatt Russell (with hat) poses with mother Goldie Hawn, father Kurt Russell and half-brother Boston Russell after his Junior-B hockey team, the Richmond Sockeyes, won the provincial championship. Canadian Press Adrian Lam

bar fights over the previous two months. He demonstrated just how far from reality he'd evidently drifted when he filmed his self-penned screenplay 2000's *Hitler Meets Christ* on the Downtown Eastside and played Hitler. Indeed, Moriarty has a passionate zeal for politics: "If I live long enough, which is questionable these days," he promised in June 2003, "yes, I will run for President of the United States in 2008."

If David Duchovny does return north of the 49th, he can rest assured that Moriarty won't be his only ex-pat neighbour. Goldie Hawn, who shot 1990's *Bird on a Wire* in town, moved into a Shaughnessy mansion in 2002 with long-time partner Kurt Russell and their son Wyatt. It was Wyatt's ability as a hockey goaltender than inspired the family's move from the exclusive southern California enclave of Pacific Palisades.

Wyatt was described by the *Prince George Citizen* as "the only player to arrive on a private jet" when he showed up to register for the Prince George Cougars' training camp in 2002. He eventually landed closer to Shaughnessy, playing for the Richmond Sockeyes Junior-B team. "There's hockey in Los Angeles, but up here, it's their church," Kurt Russell told reporters. "Wyatt could have come up and billeted with a family connected to hockey but he was just 15 turning 16 and we wanted to be with him for the last years of his high school life." Wyatt wasn't the only one on the ice. In preparation for his role in 2004's *Miracle*, playing US Olympic hockey-team coach Herb Brooks, the elder Russell took skating lessons from Wyatt's coach.

Cover Girls vs. Centrefolds

In what has to have been the most drawn-out celebrity breakup in years—Elizabeth Taylor and Richard Burton notwithstanding—Ben Affleck and Jennifer Lopez brought the "Bennifer" show to Vancouver in the summer of 2003. Renting a quiet, waterfront mansion in Deep Cove, the cuddly couple-of-the-moment could be seen at the village ice-cream parlour and strolling through the beachfront park, when not working out at Kitsilano's Executive Lifestyles or munching down appies at Yaletown's Glowbal Grill & Satay Bar.

In town to shoot director John Woo's stinkeroo thriller *Paycheck*, Affleck survived a potential "Ben Attack" when his bodyguards pounced on a set invader at Vancouver Film Studios and beat the crap out of the intruder, necessitating an airlift to Vancouver General Hospital. In mid-July, Affleck celebrated the release of *Gigli*—easily the most notoriously awful big-budget feature in recent years, starring himself and J. Lo—by hanging out sans fiancée at Brandi's Exotic Nightclub, a pricey strip bar, with actor Christian Slater, Slater's wife Ryan Haddon and actress Tara Reid. The night led to a highly publicized *National Enquirer* story immediately denied by Affleck, Haddon and Brandi's dancer Antonella "Felicia" Santini, who filed a lawsuit clarifying that she "did not engage in any sex acts with Affleck." However, Haddon said the stars did, in fact, cap the evening off with an all-night party at Haddon and Slater's rented home with several of Brandi's performers in tow.

Taking it off for Hollywood is not a new concept for Vancouver women. They've been frantically sought after by *Playboy* over the 50-year course of the magazine's existence, allegedly due in part to "the clean sea air, moist

Ladysmith, BC native Pamela Anderson in 1990 shortly before appearing as "Miss February" in *Playboy* magazine, on her way to becoming arguably the most recognizable Canadian alive. Jon Murray *The Province*

Pamela Anderson in 2000 being filmed on Vancouver set for the movie *2gether*. Arlen Redekop *The Province*

climate and healthy lifestyle" being good for skin and body tone. A more definite part of the equation is Vancouver photographer Ken Honey's sharp eye for talent. A wedding photographer by trade, Honey started taking professional shots of women as he hung out at Vancouver's nude Wreck Beach in the early sixties and went on to build a large portfolio of Playmates. Among Honey's discoveries were Dorothy Stratten (Playmate of the Year 1980, who went on to make substantial inroads in Hollywood before being murdered, at 20, by her boyfriend), Heidi Sorenson (Miss July 1981, who went on to small parts in the eighties films *History of the World: Part 1*, *Fright Night* and *Roxanne*), Kelly Tough (Miss October 1981, who slung beer mugs in the mid-1980s at North Vancouver's Avalon Pub), Kimberley Conrad (Playmate of the Year 1989, who went on to marry, have two kids with and since separate from *Playboy* founder Hugh Hefner) and Pamela Anderson.

After the JumboTron camera zoomed in on Pamela Anderson at a BC Lions game, the Vancouver fitness instructor was approached to make her modelling debut for Labatt's beer. It was Honey, though, who encouraged Anderson to move to Los Angeles by scoring her a cover shot for *Playboy* in October 1989. After having small television roles in *Married With Children* and *Home Improvement*, she hit the big time by landing the part of C.J. Parker on *Baywatch*. Due in large part to Anderson's popularity, the television show was a worldwide hit, eventually leading her to starring roles in the series *V.I.P.* and in several movies. In 1995, she entered into an on-again-off-again marriage with Mötley Crüe drummer Tommy Lee that yielded two children and a barrage of press. At the turn of the 21st century, the Ladysmith, BC, native and former Vancouver resident was arguably the world's most recognizable person, her image plastered on walls and billboards everywhere and heavily in demand via the Internet.

BACKSTAGE VANCOUVER

A century after French theatre star Sarah Bernhardt unveiled her "voice of gold" at the Vancouver Opera House in 1891, another Sarah—Halifax-born singer-songwriter Sarah McLachlan—was lighting up not only the city but the entire planet with her own gilded voice.

Discovered by Nettwerk Records at 17, she relocated to Vancouver two years later to record with the then-fledgling label. Her first two albums, 1988's *Touch* and 1991's *Solace*, solidified a strong local fan base before her third, 1993's *Fumbling Towards Ecstasy* struck triple-platinum.

In 1997, her career really took off. Her album *Surfacing* reached number two on the *Billboard* charts, sold more than seven million copies and garnered the chanteuse Grammy Awards for Best Female Pop Vocal Performance and Best Pop Instrumental Performance. The same year, McLachlan, Nettwerk co-founder Terry McBride and Sam Feldman US booking affiliate Marty Diamond launched Lilith Fair, a highly successful travelling concert featuring a revolving cast of well-known female artists including Jewel, Joan Osborne, the Pretenders' Chrissie Hynde, the Indigo Girls, Tracy Chapman, Bonnie Raitt, Missy Elliott and the Dixie Chicks. The tour cleaned up at the summer box office for three years, defying expectations of concert promoters and outselling other package shows, such as Lollapalooza. McLachlan had conquered the world as an international superstar.

In the Vancouver music industry, the first significant wave of musicians demanding international attention emerged shortly before *McCabe and Mrs. Miller* jumpstarted the city's film industry. The open-minded attitude of the late 1960s played an important role in allowing outside eyes to take notice of artists hailing from a location that wasn't Los Angeles, London, New York or Nashville.

By the latter half of the sixties, musical crossbreeding had resulted in a disparate array of genres, all of which found expression in Vancouver-spawned acts, including the hit-making Poppy Family, the blues-oriented Seeds of Time, folk rocker Tom Northcott and the psychedelicized Collectors. One evening at the Retinal Circus nightclub on Davie Street, Doors' icon Jim Morrison gushingly disclosed to Collectors' guitarist Bill Henderson how much better and more interesting Henderson's band was than Morrison's. An experimental outfit that would morph into platinum-selling rockers Chilliwack a few years later, the Collectors were as respected for singles such as "Lydia Purple" and "Looking at a Baby" as for their extended instrumental improvisations.

"A lot of the US and California bands thought the Collectors were incredible," Henderson says. "The Grateful Dead's Jerry Garcia was really into our band and Bill Graham, the San Francisco promoter, jumped up onstage at

Above: Vancouver folkie Tom Northcott was signed by Warner Brothers in the mid-1960s. He later made a living as a commercial fisherman and a lawyer. Rob Frith Collection
Right: Arguably the best Vancouver band never to hit it big, the Collectors started in 1961 as the wholesome C-Fun Classics and later morphed into Chilliwack. Rob Frith Collection

Halifax-born singer-songwriter Sarah McLachlan moved to Vancouver at 19 and based a career of international stardom here. Courtesy Nettwerk Management

the Fillmore and introduced us as 'The band that was taking rock and roll where it was going.'" The Collectors shared bills up and down the West Coast with the likes of the Dead, the Doors, Buffalo Springfield, the Steve Miller Blues Band, the Jefferson Airplane, Country Joe and the Fish, and many others. "It was a different scene back then," Henderson recalls. "I remember, one time, we went down to San Francisco to play the Fillmore with Buffalo Springfield. They wanted to leave their amps where they were on the stage and have us set up in front. That's standard procedure these days but Bill Graham said, 'No way. Nobody gets to be the big star on my stage. Everybody gets an equal shot.' That's the way a lot of people felt back then. There was a lot more sharing."

The Poppy Family formed after Saskatoon native Susan Pesklevits and the guitarist of Vancouver band the Chessmen, Terry Jacks, crossed paths on the set of CBC-TV's weekly *Music Hop*, Canada's answer to *American Bandstand*. The duo soon formed a band, married and scored a major international hit with 1970's "Which Way You Goin', Billy?" The song was the first million-selling record to come out of Vancouver, eventually moving 3.5 million copies and reaching number one in Canada, number one on US *Cashbox* chart and number two on *Billboard*. The follow-up singles, "That's Where I Went Wrong" and "Where Evil Grows," also yielded million-selling records but the couple's personal and professional union dissolved in 1972.

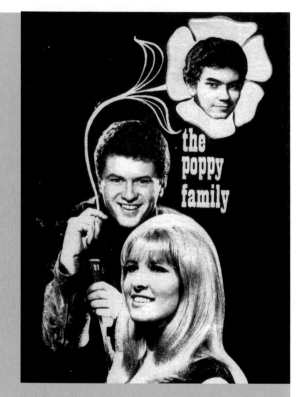

Terry and Susan Jacks of the Poppy Family, Vancouver's first million-sellers, with guitarist Craig McCaw (inset). Rob Frith Collection

An in-demand songwriter and producer by this time, Jacks, who'd had hits with acts ranging from Nana Mouskouri to Chilliwack, ensconced himself in the studio and emerged with the number one Canadian hit "Concrete Sea." But the single's success left Jacks in a quandary. "I didn't know what to put out as my next record," he says. "I had one song I'd found that had been sitting around for some time. My paperboy came by one day when I was in the midst of listening to tapes and said, 'Wow, I really like that song!' The next day, he brought his friends over to hear it and they all said, 'Yeah, is that ever a neat song!' So I thought, 'Okay, I'm going with this one.'" The song was 1973's "Seasons in the Sun," which would go on to sell 13 million copies, hitting number one worldwide. One of 10 best-selling singles of all time, it topped Canadian charts for 17 weeks and US charts for 15 weeks. The tune, however, made a circuitous route on its way to the top.

"It was originally called 'Le Moribund,' by Belgian songwriter Jacques Brel," Jacks explains. "The title means 'The Dying Man' but Brel's version was completely different. It was a funny, tongue-in-cheek song about a guy who is dying of a broken heart because his buddy is screwing his wife. Around the same time I first heard it, I'd been on the golf course with my best friend and he told me he didn't have long to live. He had acute leukemia and died four months later. I couldn't believe it. I thought, 'Man, what an awful feeling to have to tell your family and friends that you're dying.'"

'Le Moribund' had been translated into English by American poet-and-songwriter Rod McKuen and Jacks rewrote the composition to reflect his own experience. "I'd rewritten the whole song and all my friends said, 'Oh, Jacks, that sucks!'" he says with a laugh. "But people could really relate to it, whether to somebody in their family or whomever, and it had a lot of mystique. I felt the song had all the ingredients. It had catchy hooks and a melody people could remember." Indeed, it was reportedly the first record purchased by a young Kurt Cobain. Twenty years later, his band, Nirvana, performed and recorded the song.

In the meantime, an earlier West Coast musical phenomenon, the Beach Boys, gave "Seasons in the Sun" a whirl. "Al Jardine and Carl Wilson were friends of mine," says Jacks, referring to two of the band's founding members. "It was during that period, in the early seventies, when [Beach Boys' composer/leader] Brian Wilson was cracking up.

I was working in the studio a lot and they knew me, so they asked if I'd be interested in producing them. I said, 'I've got a great song for you that I've just finished writing and arranging.' I thought 'Seasons in the Sun' would be perfect for the Beach Boys. It had lyrics like 'The stars we could reach were just starfish on the beach' and the eighth-note organ line was right out of 'Good Vibrations.'

"So I went down there and stayed at Al's place," Jacks continues, "but the studio was at Brian's place. We had all the top LA musicians playing on the session, everybody was putting their voices on, Brian played the organ line and everything was coming along really well. Then Brian decided he didn't want to put his high vocal part on the track. The next thing I knew, Steve Dexter, the engineer, is saying, 'I'd better take these tapes home with me because Brian is trying to get at them.' I think Brian was pretty put out because somebody else was trying to produce the Beach Boys and it got pretty weird at his studio. In fact, I almost had a nervous breakdown. I just couldn't take the pressure of working with Brian anymore. So I went home and recorded it for my own label, Goldfish Records."

En route to the airport to catch a flight to Tahiti for a fishing holiday, Jacks dropped off an advance copy to deejay Red Robinson at Vancouver radio station CKWX. "I thought if I could get Red to play it, I could hear how it sounded on the radio in the cab on the way to the airport," says Jacks. "So we're driving along and I hear Red say, 'Terry Jacks was just here with his new record, so we'll give it a spin and see how it sounds.' I remember listening

After going number one in the world with 1974's "Seasons in the Sun," Terry Jacks wound down his performing career and founded Environment Watch. Courtesy Terry Jacks

to it in the cab, thinking, 'Oh, man, I put too much bottom end on it.' Red was the first one ever to play that record, and within four days, it was the most requested song in the country. I got a call telling me I'd better get back to town and make a deal in the States." Although Jacks was elbowed out of songwriting royalties, which were split between Brel and McKuen, he owned everything else, including the tapes, the record label and the arranging, performance and production rights.

"I knew Jacques Brel and spent time with him in Brussels shortly before he died of cancer," says Jacks of the songwriter who died in 1978, at 49. "He said, 'Man, you should be getting 50 percent of this song after all you've done for it.' But in those days, I was young, the money was pouring in from sales and I didn't really care."

In 1989, Jacks surfaced once more with the Poppy Family hit "Where Evil Grows," when perennial Vancouver punk rockers D.O.A., working with Jacks, Bryan Adams and others to bring attention to pulp-mill pollution, recorded the song as a single (and included it as a bonus track on their album *Murder*), using Jacks as producer. "I got a tour of his house," says D.O.A.'s Joe Keithley. "He said, 'You see this gold record here, Joe? This one paid for my house. You see this platinum record here? It paid for my boat.' I was like, 'Oh, so *that's* how it all works.'"

Taking Care of Business

In 1969, Winnipeg rockers the Guess Who broke internationally on the strength of hits such as "These Eyes," "Laughing," "Undun," "No Time" and "American Woman," all written or co-written by guitarist Randy Bachman.

A youthful Bruce Allen (centre) flanked by members of Bachman-Turner Overdrive (l-r) Robbie Bachman, Randy Bachman, Blair Thornton, and Fred Turner. Bruce Allen Collection

But in 1970, at the height of the band's popularity, Bachman split the fold (whether he quit or was kicked out depends on who you ask). Starting from scratch again wouldn't be easy.

"There was a loose-knit organization of booking agents across Canada that swapped acts back and forth," says Bruce Allen. "When Randy left the Guess Who, their manager was powerful enough to tell other booking agents, 'If you book Randy Bachman, you'll never book the Guess Who again.' Everybody from Calgary east supported the boycott. They had to, if they wanted to stay in business. So Randy came to me because I was by myself out here in Vancouver. If his new band Brave Belt [consisting of his brother Robbie, ex-Guess Who bandmate Chad Allan and Fred Turner] came out here, I could put them in the clubs to earn money— places like Image One, Mumbles, Sneaky Pete's, Big Pussycat, Pharaoh's, the Cave, the Breakers—and he could pour his earnings into making a record. He convinced the rest of the band to pick up and move to Vancouver."

Brave Belt released two albums but neither burned up the charts. Nevertheless, the quartet, and Allen, persevered. "Randy kept recording relentlessly," says Allen. "Finally, we started shopping what was supposed to be Brave Belt's third album but all the record companies turned us down." Twenty-five labels reportedly passed on the product before Chicago-based Mercury Records telephoned Bachman to express interest. When the label rep flew to Vancouver to check out the band, Allen booked the quartet into the Cave and "packed the place with as many people as I could get in the door." The rep was impressed but didn't like the name. "We were driving around and saw this trucker magazine called *Overdrive*," says Allen. "They thought it would make a good name, so they called the band Bachman-Turner Overdrive: BTO."

Content with his part in the coup, Allen was ready to return to his booking agency. "That's when Randy came to me and said, 'I'm going to need a manager and I want you to manage the band.'" Allen was reluctant to take on a new occupation with a steep learning curve but eventually caved in, deciding to begin his education by hitting the road with the band. In order to keep the booking business running while he was away, Allen enlisted independent booking agent Sam Feldman to join forces with him. "I went to Sam and said, 'I need some help. Why don't you pool your bands with mine and I'll make you a deal.'" The deal he made with Feldman, which exists to this day between Bruce Allen Talent and S.L. Feldman & Associates, was a 50-50 split.

In 1973, the band and its manager set off to conquer North America, in a rental car. "Randy didn't want to go by bus," says Allen, "so we rented cars to save money. We had one roadie driving an equipment van and we went around the continent many, many times that way. We'd be on the road 10

Vancouver booking agent Bruce Allen reluctantly agreed to become manager of Bachman-Turner Overdrive, but after BTO scored a string of hits he had no reason to regret his career change. Bruce Allen Collection

or 11 months out of the year. That's how we broke the BTO." The band scored hit after hit for the next five years: "Takin' Care of Business," "You Ain't Seen Nothing Yet," "Let It Ride," "Hey You," "Lookin' Out for No. 1," "Roll on Down the Highway." Another Bachman brother, Tim, had replaced Chad Allan after the second Brave Belt album but was replaced by guitarist Blair Thornton after the first two BTO albums; Randy bowed out in 1978. "Bachman-Turner Overdrive was the biggest band ever to come out of this country," asserts Allen. "They nailed AM radio, FM radio and sold tickets like there was no tomorrow. We set records for the fastest stadium and arena sellouts in history that remained unbroken until New Kids on the Block or whatever came along."

In the late seventies, a larger-than-life musical guru arrived in Vancouver, who was associated with many of the biggest acts in the world. Highly influential British blues vocalist Long John Baldry (so designated because of his six-foot-seven-inch frame) had mentored Elton John, Rod Stewart, the Rolling Stones' Mick Jagger and Charlie Watts, the Yardbirds' Eric Clapton and Jimmy Page, Cream's Jack Bruce and Ginger Baker, and countless other British musicians in the early 1960s. By the late 1970s, however, "he hated England," says Les Wiseman, and decided to immigrate to Canada. "He came to Canada, decided Toronto was not where it was at and subsequently moved to Vancouver."

Baldry stayed pals with erstwhile protegés Stewart and John and was immortalized in Sir Elton's 1975 Top-10 hit "Someone Saved My Life Tonight," referred to as "Sugar Bear." John, who had played keyboards in Baldry's backing band Bluesology in 1966 (under his real name, Reg Dwight) was engaged to be married in the late sixties and had become deeply depressed over the matter. (He didn't reveal his bisexuality until 1976.) Fearing for his well-being, Baldry took John and his songwriting partner Bernie Taupin on a marathon drinking binge and convinced the singer/pianist to break off the engagement. Although lyrically veiled, John has since affirmed that the incident chronicled in the song is all-too-true and credits Baldry with rescuing him from the brink of suicide.

Left: Future stars Ron Wood (left), and Keith Richards (right) both played with Long John Baldry earlier in their careers. Dee Lippingwell

Opposite: Musical guru Long John Baldry mentored Eric Clapton, Elton John and Mick Jagger before moving to Vancouver in the late 1970s. Dee Lippingwell

When Long John Baldry's keyboardist Reg Dwight decided to go solo, he combined Baldry's first name with that of band saxophonist Elton Dean to make up new stage name Elton John. At left, Elton rips up the Pacific Coliseum in 1975.
Dee Lippingwell

Baldry continues to reside in Vancouver and became a Canadian citizen in 1980. In January 2001, he celebrated his 60th birthday with a sold-out show at the Commodore Ballroom. Entirely by coincidence, another swinging sixties British scene-maker, former Rolling Stones' manager and producer Andrew Loog Oldham, also settled in Vancouver in the early 2000s.

Working for the Weekend

The American music industry also found Vancouver to be a mighty hospitable place during the 1980s, a bona fide phenomenon that traces its somewhat unlikely roots to a quintet of red-leather-clad lads with the name of Loverboy. Like BTO, the band conquered North America under the tutelage of Bruce Allen.

After the demise of BTO, Lou Blair, former proprietor of Oil Can Harry's and Ziggy's Sidedoor in Vancouver and then with the Refinery in Calgary, convinced a skeptical Allen to check out a new group consisting of singer Mike Reno, guitarist Paul Dean, keyboardist Doug Johnson, bassist Scott Smith and drummer Matt Frenette. Allen agreed to take them on and inked a deal with CBS Canada but the band had a very rough start. "It was horrible, just

Guitarist Paul Dean of Loverboy, the second Vancouver group to conquer North America under the tutelage of Bruce Allen. Dee Lippingwell

Singer Mike Reno (right) and guitarist Paul Dean (left) of Loverboy. Manager Bruce Allen at first thought them "fucking horrible." Dee Lippingwell

fucking horrible," recalls Allen. The band made a habit of bombing whenever US label reps happened to be in the audience but Allen finally persuaded Columbia Records that they'd improve once they were put on the road. "We worked and worked and worked, and the second album blew the roof off. It became a monster hit in 1981 with 'Working for the Weekend.' Those first two Loverboy records were the first records Bruce Fairbairn and Bob Rock ever produced. I talked them into producing Loverboy as a favour and that was their start as a team."

Bruce Fairbairn, who had played trumpet and produced albums for Vancouver rockers Prism, picked up a Producer of the Year Juno in 1980 for his work with the group. Rock, meanwhile, had been guitarist in the Payola$, working at Little Mountain Sound by day, as an engineer. Together and apart, the pair produced the hardest-rocking mainstream acts of the late 1980s, including Aerosmith, Van Halen, AC/DC, Mötley Crüe, Metallica, The Cult and Bon Jovi, whose

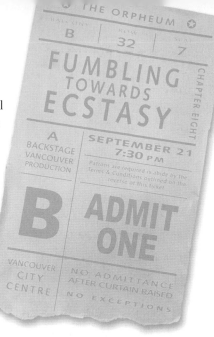

James Hetfield and Metallica logged a lot of time recording with producer Bob Rock in Vancouver—until they made him enough money to build a new studio in Hawaii.
Dee Lippingwell

1986 album *Slippery When Wet* broke the duo internationally. Along with Zambian-born, British-based Robert John "Mutt" Lange (now Mr. Shania Twain and the producer of several Bryan Adams albums), Fairbairn and Rock were the hottest rock producers on the planet during the late 1980s and well into the 1990s.

"To have two of the biggest producers in the world come from Vancouver and have the other one working with one of Vancouver's biggest artists is absolutely phenomenal," says Allen, who handled the business end of Fairbairn's career until the latter's death in May 1999, at 49. "Bruce Fairbairn was a funny guy," Allen continues. "He always found a place for a trumpet on all the records he produced, just so he could play some trumpet. He was really creatively artistic and would go outside the rock realm to find weird instruments to use on albums, like bagpipes or glockenspiels. Bruce Fairbairn believed, like Sam Phillips believed, that you have to catch the artists in the studio as they're playing live. Fairbairn wanted to hear the groove and get locked into it.

Vancouver superstar Bryan Adams onstage in 1986. In three years Adams progressed from replacement vocalist in local band Sweeney Todd to US platinum with 1983's "Cuts Like a Knife." Dee Lippingwell

"Bob Rock, on the other hand, is an engineer; he likes everything to be technically excellent. So Bruce and Bob working together was a great team because Bob could get the sounds and Bruce, being the producer, could overrule him when he felt he'd captured the band's performance. After maybe three or four takes, he'd say, 'That'll work.' With Rock, it would be 40 takes and maybe it still ain't right. At which point, he'd start cutting things up and splicing them back together to make it work. That was the difference: Fairbairn was all about the vibe, while Bob was all about getting the right sounds and the technical stuff by setting up microphones in a certain way and tweaking the sounds to make things perfect.

"The thing was, Fairbairn could tell you the day he went into the studio how much the album was going to cost, the day the album was going to be finished and the day the album was going to be mastered. If Bruce said it was going to be $200,000, then that's what it would be. If he said he'd have it August 15, then that's when you'd get it. If Bob, on the other hand, said the record was going to be $200,000, it would end up being $400,000. If he said you'd get it August 15, then you'd get it the following June."

Native Son

In 1980, a North Shore teenager named Bryan Adams, fresh from replacing vocalist Nick Gilder in local glam-rockers Sweeney Todd, had been hammering on Allen's office door. "For six weeks, he was trying to get a meeting to talk to me," says Allen. "And I thought, 'Jesus Christ, "Let Me Take You Dancing." Are you fucking kidding?'," referring to Adams's first solo hit, a disco-ish ditty released in 1979. Adams's sights, however, were set on much bigger things. He had begun writing and recording demos with ex-Prism member Jim Vallance, a fruitful collaboration that lasted until 1989. "He had some pull at the clubs," recalls Allen, "so I put him in places like the Body Shop downtown and Whispers in North Van and went to see him. He was so fucking relentless, I finally said 'Okay.'"

Adams's second album, *You Want It, You Got It* (working title: *Bryan Adams Hasn't Heard of You, Either*) was released in 1981 and warranted the rocker a warm-up slot the following year on tours with Foreigner and the Kinks. The latter band's guitarist, Dave Davies, mistook Adams for a roadie. Following the release of 1983's *Cuts Like a Knife*, no such mistakes would be made again. The title track proved a hit and the album went US platinum, entering the *Billboard* Top 10. In 1984, *Reckless* fared even better, eventually hitting number one on the album charts in August 1985 and yielding hit after hit: "Run to You," "Somebody," "Heaven," "Kids Wanna Rock" and "Summer of '69." That same year, Tina Turner joined Adams in the studio for the duet "It's Only Love," yet another chart-topper.

"Bryan had gotten pretty big in America but he wanted to be big all over the world," says Allen. "But touring the rest of the world was new to me. So I thought, 'We'll do it the same way we did it in America, by getting on as the warm-up act on somebody else's tour.' Well, nobody would put us on their tour because Adams was too big. Then I thought, 'Hey, we've got this duet with Tina Turner. Why don't we ask Tina?' At that point, her career was nothing in North America. She was playing cabarets and lounges, but in Europe, she was playing arenas. So while Bryan's career was ascending in the States, we decided to go to Europe and open for Tina Turner for $1,500 a night, whereas we were making $15,000 a night in North America.

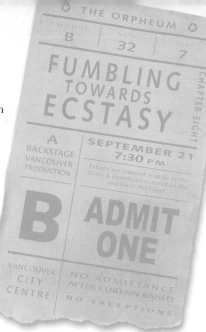

With no support from his record label, Adams embarked on a 30-date European tour, opening for the formidable soul singer. "We made the deal, we went over there, we opened for her," says Allen. "Nobody knew who the fuck we were, but when Bryan joined her onstage three-quarters of the way through her set to do 'It's Only Love,' it was like she was putting her stamp of approval on him, and she's queen over there. If there were 15,000 people in the audience, we may have got 1,500 of them. We built his career outside of North America around that."

In Vancouver, Adams is known for his devotion to local heritage. In the late 1980s, he campaigned against the demolition of the Georgia Medical Building, a fetching art-deco structure in the heart of the city, and in the early 1990s he purchased the century-old Oppenheimer Brothers Warehouse at 100 Powell, on the edge of Gastown. Named after the grocery wholesaling firm owned by the city's second mayor, David Oppenheimer, the original two-storey structure was erected in 1891 with a third storey added in 1916. Refurbishing the red-brick edifice entailed several years, several architects and a reported $6 million, though at least a portion of the cost went to installing the Warehouse, Adams's state-of-the-art recording studio, which has been booked by the likes of Sarah McLachlan, R.E.M., AC/DC, Nine Inch Nails and Elton John.

You Want It, You Got It

It might have taken the better part of a century, but by the 1990s, Vancouver had transformed itself from a city known for importing world-class performers to one that was exporting them by the bushel. Although long considered a trampoline to Tinseltown, the old mill settlement had matured and established itself as an international HQ from which stars could not only further their careers but also live, work and play.

S.L. Feldman and Associates, the music management and booking empire headed by Bruce Allen's long-time partner Sam Feldman, expanded into the film and television arenas in the 1990s with the Characters Talent Agency, representing some of the country's top actors, directors, composers and producers. The company's music division, meanwhile, added platinum-selling artists Joni Mitchell, Diana Krall, the Chieftains, Norah Jones and the Tragically Hip to its roster. Allen continued to manage rocker Bryan Adams, while adding Canadian songbird Anne Murray, country chanteuse Martina McBride and crooning heartthrob Michael Bublé to his stable. Nettwerk Management, an offshoot of the phenomenally successful Nettwerk Records label—propelled in no small way by the mega-success of Sarah McLachlan—took on the astronomical careers of Avril Lavigne, the Barenaked Ladies, Dido, Our Lady Peace, Chantal Kreviazuk, Sum 41, Swollen Members and the Stereophonics.

During the latter half of the 1990s, local hard-rock station CFOX was instrumental in supporting independent albums by the Matthew Good Band and Nickelback, setting the stage for the two clients of Burnaby's Greenhouse Studios to go onto bigger things. After releasing one of the most successful independent debuts in Canadian history, *Last of the Ghetto Astronauts*, the Matthew Good Band also recorded their second album, *Underdogs*, at home on their own budget. Bolstered by a distribution deal from A&M, the record went platinum and earned them the Best New Group Juno at the Canadian Music Awards. Their next album, *Beautiful Midnight*, won them Junos for best group and best rock album.

Enthusiastic local airplay encouraged Nickelback to soldier through one EP and one album that received little national attention before their third independent album, *The State*, took off in 2000 to the extent that major labels in both Canada and the US picked it up and eventually sold more than half a million copies. Their third album, *Silver Side Up*, sold more than nine million copies worldwide and featured "How You Remind Me," the first single by a Canadian band to hit number one status in both Canada and the US since the Guess Who's "American Woman."

Opposite: Tina Turner, one of the most erotic performers in pop, turns on another Vancouver audience in 1977. She kept this up into her sixties.
Dee Lippingwell

Above: Chad Kroeger and Nickelback consolidated Vancouver's reputation as a pop music hot spot when they were named North America's Number One Most Played Rock Artist in 2002. Arlen Redekop *The Province*

Right: Coquitlam's Matthew Good was a hard-touring folk troubadour before turning things around with a big guitar sound in the 1990s. Dee Lippingwell

Opposite: The city of Nanaimo did a lot to shake its reputation as BC's capital of bad taste when it gave the world the sophisticated jazz pianist and vocalist Diana Krall, whose 2001 release, *The Look of Love*, went quintuple platinum. Courtesy Sam Feldman

After two more successful singles, "Too Bad" and "Never Again," the band was named North America's Number One Most Played Rock Artist of 2002.

The group's name is highly representative of their caffeine-crazed home base: "After recording our first songs, we still didn't have a name. I was working as a cashier at Starbucks Coffee and let's just say … coffee was $1.45," explains bassist Mike Kroeger. In the wake of a triumphant world tour, Nickelback frontman Chad Kroeger returned home to produce and co-write songs for local band Default and teamed with entertainment attorney Jonathan Simkin to found 604Records, signing other Vancouver up-and-comers such as Theory of a Deadman. Kroeger even reached out to collaborate with the staunchly independent Mint Records, which attracted worldwide attention around the same time, thanks to its critically acclaimed acts Neko Case and the New Pornographers.

But none of Vancouver's unprecedented domestic success indicates that major players have stopped coming to Vancouver from elsewhere. In the spring of 2004 alone, Donald Sutherland, Jennifer Garner, Wesley Snipes, Christian Slater, Kevin Spacey, Morgan Freeman, Diane Lane, Robert Loggia, Colm Feore, Angie Harmon, Ryan

Phillippe, Justin Timberlake and LL Cool J were all in town filming various projects, while recording artists R.E.M., k.d. lang, Billy Joel, the Cranberries, Seal, Yes, Metallica, KISS and AC/DC had made recent forays to pump up the volume in local studios.

In Sarah Bernhardt's day, Vancouver's role in world-class entertainment was little more than a muddy stop that happened to have an opera house. Today, the city is a thriving international cultural centre in its own right, boasting extremely prominent players such as Adams, Allen, Nettwerk and Nickelback. And, of course, there is the Sarah of today, who can't imagine living anywhere else. "I love Vancouver," McLachlan says. "I've been all over the world and nothing is finer than Vancouver, BC, Canada. It's a very inspiring place."

She is not the only one who feels that way.

Sarah McLachlan 2004
Courtesy Kharen Hill Nettwerk Management

ACKNOWLEDGEMENTS

The authors are immensely grateful and indebted to the following individuals for sharing their time, memories and anecdotes with us for inclusion in this book: Bruce Allen, Denny Boyd, Janet Forsyth, Terry Jacks, Joe Keithley, John Mackie, Bill Millerd, Terry David Mulligan, Hugh Pickett, Don Prior, Dal Richards, Peter Trower and Les Wiseman. We would also like to thank the families of the late Jack Cullen and Monty McFarlane for allowing us unrestricted access to their archives. Special thanks to Chuck Davis, author and demon researcher, whose exhaustive work filled in many a pothole along the road. Posthumous appreciation goes to Ivan Ackery, whose memoir, *Fifty Years on Theatre Row* (Hancock House, 1980), added colour to an otherwise sketchy outline of Vancouver's early years of entertainment.

The authors would also like to thank the photographers who were in the right place at the right time with the lens cap off, specifically Ralph Bower, Craig Hodge and Dee Lippingwell. Special thanks to photo researcher Gary Olsen, who spent days poring over files with the fine folk at the Vancouver City Archives and the Vancouver Public Library.

Greg Potter would like to thank his family for their gracious, forgiving and enduring support. Also, Victor Bonderoff, Mark Fancher, Jill Lambert, Frances Potter, Justin Smallbridge, Howard White and Silas White for reading drafts and offering invaluable suggestions; Bonnie Bowman and John Moore for their sunny cynicism and hysterical correspondence; Peter Trower and Jim Christy for inspiration and encouragement; Les Wiseman for teaching the tactics of trench warfare; and, of course, Red Robinson, whose initial phone call sparked the notion in the first place and whose unwavering enthusiasm stoked the fire.

Red Robinson would like to thank Craig Hodge, a good friend and former photographer with *The Columbian* newspaper, who went out of his way to assist with photographs; radio archivist Jim Morrison, who unearthed some singularly historic photographs; S.L. Feldman & Associates, who assisted in locating key photos; Phil Mackesy for taking the time to process the images onto disc; Bruce Allen and his staff for their cooperation; Terry McBride for his courtesy in providing a stunning photo of Sarah McLachlan; Hugh Pickett for his personal involvement in selecting photos from his unbelievable collection of memorabilia; Michael J. Fox and his mother Phyllis for their invitation to dinner and the personal notes from Michael; Randy Bachman for his nice words about Greg and myself; and Art Jones, for granting access to his personal photographic collection. Special mention to Sev Morin, one-time owner of the Gai Paree supper club in Burnaby, who opened some special doors during this project. A special bow also to the Vancouver Public Library, the Pacific Newspaper Group, the City of Vancouver Archives, and the City of Coquitlam Heritage Photos for their very special photos. Finally, a big round of applause for all the celebrities who grace these pages.

Published by
Harbour Publishing Co. Ltd.
P.O. Box 219
Madeira Park, BC
V0N 2H0
www.harbourpublishing.com

Edited by Silas White
Image research and photo editing by Vici Johnstone
Cover and text design by Roger Handling
Cover photographs: Elvis Presley courtesy Red Robinson Collection; Marilyn Monroe courtesy Monty McFarlane Collection; Interior Vancouver Opera House, City of Vancouver Archives Bu P389; Sarah McLachlan courtesy Kharen Hill Nettwerk Management; Orpheum on Granville 1946, City of Vancouver Archives CVA 1184-2290.
Image on page 1, Chief Dan George, Vancouver Public Library VPL 44651; page 2, posters, Vancouver Public Library VPL 7333; page 3, Orpheum on Granville 1946, City of Vancouver Archives CVA 1184-2290; page 5, Frank Sinatra, Craig Hodge.

Printed and bound in Canada

Harbour Publishing acknowledges financial support from the Government of Canada through the Book Publishing Industry Development Program and the Canada Council for the Arts, and from the Province of British Columbia through the British Columbia Arts Council and the Book Publisher's Tax Credit through the Ministry of Provincial Revenue.

Library and Archives Canada Cataloguing in Publication

Potter, Greg (Gregory Ernest)
   Backstage Vancouver: a century of entertainment legends / Greg Potter, Red Robinson.

Includes index.
ISBN 1-55017-334-0

   1. Entertainers—British Columbian—Vancouver—History—Anecdotes. I. Robinson, Red II. Title.

PN2306.V3P68 2004   791'.092'20971133   C2004-903104-X

INDEX

PHOTO CREDITS

Front cover photographs: Elvis Presley courtesy Red Robinson Collection; Marilyn Monroe courtesy Monty McFarlane Collection; Interior Vancouver Opera House, City of Vancouver Archives Bu P389; Sarah McLaclan courtesy Kharen Hill Nettwerk Management; Orpheum on Granville 1946, Jack Lindsay photo, City of Vancouver Archives, CVA 1184-2290.

Back cover photographs: The Beatles courtesy Red Robinson Collection; Yvonne De Carlo, MPTV.net; Pamela Anderson, Jon Murray *The Province*.

Author photographs: Greg Potter, Mark Fancher; Red Robinson, Staccie Braken-Horrocks.

Bruce Allen Collection pp. 156, 170, 171; Ralph Bower photos pp. 70, 75, 151; Rob Frith Collection pp. 128, 166 (both), 168; Courtesy Sam Feldman pp. 160, 183; Craig Hodge photos pp. 5, 10, 73, 134, 135 (left); Dee Lippingwell pp. 8-9, 124, 125, 126, 127, 132, 133, 135 (right), 136, 139, 140 (top), 143, 146, 147, 148, 159, 172, 173, 174-175, 176 (both), 177, 178-179, 180, 182 (right); Monty McFarlane collection pp. 67 (right), 105; MPTV.net pp. 24, 80; Hugh Pickett collection pp. 42 (top), 52 (both), 56, 57; Dal Richards collection pp. 61, 62, 63, 74 (right), 78, 79 (left), 112; Red Robinson collection pp. 6, 12 (top), 68, 79 (right), 88, 90-91, 92 (both), 93, 94, 95, 96, 97, 98, 99, 100, 101, 102 (both), 103, 120, 121, 129 (bottom), 142; Other Collections p. 1 Gordon F. Sedawie photo, *The Province*, Vancouver Public Library, VPL 44651; p. 2 Vancouver Public Library, VPL 7333; p. 3 Jack Lindsay photo, City of Vancouver Archives, CVA 1184-2290; p. 7 Ross J. Kenward photo, *The Province*, Vancouver Public Library, VPL S-69069; p. 12 (bottom) William H. Cunningham photo, *The Province*, Vancouver Public Library, VPL S-60081; p. 13 (top) Wayne Leidenfrost photo, *The Province*; p. 13 (bottom) Stuart Thomson photo, City of Vancouver Archives, CVA 99-2790; p. 14 Bill Keay photo, *Vancouver Sun*; p. 15 Bill Keay photo, *Vancouver Sun*; p. 16 *Vancouver Sun*; p. 18 City of Vancouver Archives, Bu P438; p. 19 Frederick G. Goodenough photo, City of Vancouver Archives, Bu P397; p. 20 City of Vancouver Archives, Bu P389; p. 21 (top) City of Vancouver Archives, Port P1376; p. 21 (bottom) Vancouver Public Library, VPL 7333; p. 22 Frederick G. Goodenough photo, City of Vancouver Archives, Bu P134.3; p. 23 Vancouver Public Library, VPL S-22311; p. 25 Jack Lindsay photo, City of Vancouver Archives, Bu P479.1; p. 27 City of Vancouver Archives, Bu P440; p. 28 City of Vancouver Archives, CVA 470-22; p. 29 W. J. Moore photo, City of Vancouver Archives, Port N100; p. 30 Jack Lindsay photo, City of Vancouver Archives, CVA 1184-2306; p. 31 *Vancouver Sun*; p. 32 *The Province*, Vancouver Public Library, VPL 59307; p. 33 Jack Lindsay photo, City of Vancouver Archives, CVA 1184-2229; pp. 34-35 King Studio, Vancouver Public Library, VPL S-70488; p. 36 Jack Lindsay photo, City of Vancouver Archives, CVA 1184-2290; p. 37 (left) Ian Lindsay photo, *Vancouver Sun*; p. 37 (right) Steve Bosch, *Vancouver Sun*; p. 38 (top) Jack Lindsay photo, City of Vancouver Archives, CVA 1184-524; p. 38 (bottom) Jack Lindsay photo; City of Vancouver Archives, CVA 1184-517; p. 39 Jack Lindsay photo, City of Vancouver Archives, CVA 1184-529; p. 42 (bottom) Jack Lindsay photo, City of Vancouver Archives, CVA 1184-1963; p. 43 Stuart Thomson photo, Vancouver Public Library, VPL 11025; p. 45 (both) Hugh Pickett collection, *Vancouver Sun*; p. 46 *Vancouver Sun*; p. 48 Jack Lindsay photo, City of Vancouver Archives, CVA 1184-400; p. 49 David Boswell; p. 50 Colin Price, *The Province*; p. 51 BC Entertainment Hall of Fame; p. 53 Sev Morin collection; p. 55 William H. Cunningham photo, *The Province*, Vancouver Public Library, VPL S-59973; p. 58 Hugh Pickett collection, *Vancouver Sun*; p. 60 Jack Lindsay photo, City of Vancouver Archives, CVA 1184-2313; p. 64 Stuart Thomson photo, City of Vancouver Archives, CVA 99-2742; p. 65 Ken Oakes, *Vancouver Sun*; p. 66 David H. Buchan; p. 67 (left) Deni Eagland, *Vancouver Sun*; p. 69 Art Jones, Vancouver Public Library, VPL 80676-A; p. 71 William H. Cunningham, *The Province*, Vancouver Public Library, VPL S-61220; p. 72 William H. Cunningham, *The Province*, Vancouver Public Library, VPL 59767; p. 74 (left) courtesy Eleanor Vallee; p. 76 *Vancouver Sun*; p. 77 Henry Fox; p. 82 Courtesy the Ridge Theatre; p. 83 (both) Courtesy Coquitlam Heritage Photos; p. 84 Harry Filion, *Vancouver Sun*; p. 85 Robert E. Olsen photo, *The Province*, Vancouver Public Library, VPL 60436A; p. 86 *The Province*, Vancouver Public Library, VPL S-59452; p. 89 Artray Ltd. photo, Vancouver Public Library, VPL 82431; p. 104 William H. Cunningham photo, *The Province*, Vancouver Public Library, VPL 62485; p. 107 Deni Eagland *Vancouver Sun*; p. 108 Eric W. Cable photo, *The Province*, Vancouver Public Library, VPL 60584; p. 110 Jack Lindsay photo, City of Vancouver Archives, CVA 1184-3470; p. 111 David C. Paterson photo, *The Province* Vancouver Public Library, VPL 40652; p. 114 Peter Hulbert, *Vancouver Sun*; p. 115 Ian Lindsay, *Vancouver Sun*; p. 116 John Denniston, *The Province*; p. 117 Leonard Frank photo, Vancouver Public Library, VPL 53715; p. 118 Croton Studio photo, Vancouver Public Library, VPL 80377; p. 119 Deni Eagland, *Vancouver Sun*; p. 122 Harold Coppin photo, Red Robinson Collection; p. 129 (top) Ian Lindsay *Vancouver Sun*; p. 130 Les Vogt Collection; p. 138 Steve Bosch, *Vancouver Sun*; p. 140 Stuart Davis, *Vancouver Sun*; p. 144 Peter Battistoni, *Vancouver Sun*; p. 145 Peter Battistoni, *Vancouver Sun*; p. 153 Copyright 2004 Alan Zenuk Universal Television Networks; pp. 154-155 Wayne Leidenfrost *The Province*; p. 157 Roy Luckow; p. 158 Gerry Kahrmann, *Vancouver Sun*; p. 161 Colin Price, *The Province*, p. 162 Adrian Lam, Canadian Press; p. 163 Jon Murray, *The Province*; p. 164 Arlen Redekop, *The Province*; p. 167 Courtesy Nettwerk Management; p. 169 Courtesy Terry Jacks; p. 182 (left) Arlen Redekop, *The Province*; p. 184 Courtesy Kharen Hill Nettwerk Management; front endsheet Jack Lindsay photo, City of Vancouver Archives, CVA 1184-2285; back endsheet Vancouver Public Library, VPL 11037.

MORE GREAT READING

Yours, Al: The Collected Letters of Al Purdy
Edited by Sam Solecki

In this fascinating and funny collection of correspondence that spans over 50 years, Canada's greatest poet lets it all hang out in spirited private exchanges with Pierre Trudeau, Carol Shields, Earle Birney, Anna Porter, Charles Bukowski, Margaret Laurence, Margaret Atwood, Michael Ondaatje, Gwendolyn MacEwan, Jack McClelland, Northrup Frye and many other notables.
ISBN 1-55017-332-4 • 6 x 9 • 560 pages • hardcover

Rafe: A Memoir
Rafe Mair

In this intimate and intriguing memoir, Rafe Mair uncovers behind-the-scenes exploits during his 15 years practicing law in Vancouver and Kamloops, his five eventful years in Bill Bennett's provincial government, and his nearly 25 years as a radio broadcaster.
ISBN 1-55017-319-7 • 6 x 9 • 304 pages • hardcover

Raincoast Chronicles 20: Lilies & Fireweed: Frontier Women of British Columbia
Stephen Hume

Raincoast Chronicles 20: Lilies & Fireweed is packed with unforgettable stories and amazing historical photographs of women surviving in the unforgiving, sometimes hostile environment of pioneer and aboriginal British Columbia. From hospitals to dance halls, classrooms to cannery floors, this pictorial essay shows how women helped build BC.
ISBN 1-55017-326-X • 8½ x 11 • 80 pages • b&w photographs • paperback

The Remarkable Adventures of Portuguese Joe Silvey
Jean Barman

British Columbia is known for the colourful pioneers who helped build and shape the character of this weird but wonderful province. And few were as colourful as Portuguese Joe Silvey—a saloon keeper, whaler and pioneer of seine fishing in British Columbia. Filled with historical photographs, this book brings the BC frontier to life.
ISBN 1-55017-326-X • 8½ x 11 • 80 pages • b&w photographs • paperback

Raincoast Chronicles 19: Stories and History of the British Columbia Coast
Edited by Howard White

Since the first Raincoast Chronicles was published in 1972, this series has become perennial favourite with its funny, fiery depiction of British Columbia's past. In this issue, the fascinating history of squatters in Vancouver, BC is unveiled, fishing superstitions are explained, and you learn why crows make lousy pets.
ISBN 1-55017-316-2 • 8½ x 11 • 80 pages • b&w photographs • paperback

Tong: The Story of Tong Louie, Vancouver's Quiet Titan
E.G. Perrault

Tong Louie, son of wholesaler H.Y. Louie, grew up in Vancouver at a time when some of his clients wouldn't let a Chinese man walk through their front door and died one of the wealthiest men in British Columbia. Along the way, the owner of London Drugs and IGA in BC became a bridge between the Chinese and non-Chinese communities in Vancouver. Filled with historical photographs, this book shows Vancouver in a new light.
ISBN 1-55017-231-X • 10 x 10 • 180 pages • b&w and colour photographs • hardcover

The Encyclopedia of British Columbia

Editorial Director, Daniel Francis

Ten years in the making, the *EBC* is a luxurious full-colour volume that touches every fact of BC from the formation of the Coast Mountains to the development of the Ballard Fuel cell to the colourful politicians, artists, writers and entertainers who call BC home.

ISBN 1-55017-200-X • 8½ x 11 • 824 pages • 1000+ photographs, maps and illustrations • hardcover

MORE GREAT PHOTOGRAPHY BOOKS FROM HARBOUR PUBLISHING

Birds of the Raincoast: Habits and Habitat

Harvey Thommasen and Kevin Hutchings with Wayne Campbell and Mark Hume *Birds of the Raincoast* represents the next step in West Coast bird books, a treasury of exceptional, large-format photographs with an informative text that moves beyond simple identification to probe deeper into the lives of our feathered friends. It examines birds in their environments, noting what they do, and where and when they can be found.

ISBN 1-55017-300-6 • 8½ x 11 • 224 pages • colour photographs • hardcover

The Wild Edge: Clayoquot, Long Beach and Barkley Sound

Jacqueline Windh

Jacqueline Windh has spent ten years photographing the Clayoquot-Pacific Rim in all its seasons and moods, studying its history and getting to know its people. In *The Wild Edge* she shares her findings in images and words, supplementing her unforgettable scenic photographs with a light-hearted but informative text that blends history and science with essential visitor guidance.

ISBN 1-55017-350-2 • 8½ x 11 • 168 pages • colour photographs • hardcover

Natural Light: Visions of British Columbia

David Nunuk

British Columbia's beauty has inspired many photo collections but none quite like David Nunuk's. From frosted mountain peaks to the low-lying farmlands of the Fraser Valley, from the Sahara-like sand dunes of Farwell Canyon to the dripping moss-bedecked rainforest of the Queen Charlotte Islands, the photographs in *Natural Light* capture the drama of British Columbia in a whole new light.

ISBN 1-55017-273-5 • 14 x 11 • 120 pages • 120 colour photographs • hardcover

Bella Coola: Life in the Heart of the Coast Mountains

Hans Granander and Michael Wigle

The Bella Coola Valley lies in the misty heart of British Columbia's West Coast, where the Pacific spills into the forest-clad cracks in the Coast Mountains. Through their light-hearted text and breathtaking photographs, Michael Wigle and Hans Granander introduce you to this wild country, its residents, animals and stunning beauty.

ISBN 1-55017-305-7 • 8½ x 11 • 160 pages • 160 colour photos • hardcover

Visions of the Wild: A Voyage by Kayak Around Vancouver Island

Maria Coffey and Dag Goering

Brimming with breathtaking colour photos and compelling journal entries, an inspiring chronicle of the adventure of a lifetime.

ISBN 1-55017-264-6 • 8 x 9½ • 192 pages • colour photos • hardcover